The Grouse

ARTISTS' IMPRESSIONS

The Grouse

ARTISTS' IMPRESSIONS

SWAN·HILL
PRESS

Above
GROUSE IN YORKSHIRE
Rodger McPhail
Oil

Alnwick Castle,
Northumberland.
NE66 1NG
Telephone: 01665 602456
Fax: 01665 606122

No game bird in the world is as revered as the Red Grouse – a wild, exciting and unique inhabitant of Britain's beautiful heather moors. Together with his beautiful cousins, the Black Grouse (our very own bird of paradise), the desperately endangered Capercaillie and the hardy Ptarmigan, grouse engender passions amongst sportsmen and conservationists alike.

To create this book, Simon Gudgeon and other great modern sporting artists worked together on a project in which they share a great passion. The result is a magical and fascinating insight into the way that different artists view and depict their subject. The passion runs through every page of the book and it will surely grace the coffee table of anyone who has encountered this family of very special game birds and has any interest in sporting or wildlife art.

Duke of Northumberland

Copyright ©2007 Simon Gudgeon, Ashley Boon, Ben Hoskyns,
Terence Lambert, Rodger McPhail, Derek Robertson,
Jonathan Sainsbury, Keith Sykes, Owen Williams

First published in the UK in 2007
by Swan Hill Press, an imprint of Quiller Publishing Ltd

British Library Cataloguing-in-Publication Data
A catalogue record for this book is available from the British Library

ISBN 978 1 84689 019 2

Printed in China
Design by Giraffic Design

Swan Hill Press

An imprint of Quiller Publishing Ltd
Wykey House, Wykey, Shrewsbury SY4 1JA
Tel: 01939 261616 Fax: 01939 261606
E-mail: info@quillerbooks.com
Website: www.countrybooksdirect.com

CONTENTS

blue gloss on
rump &
couts esp.
in strong
sunlight

umber
primaries
+ tail

white tail
edges
on couts
not
rectrices

vermiculation
on all feathers
terminating
in white
edges on
chest —
other feathers
end in
ochre

Red Grouse Sketches
Glen Esk.
July - bright day
with showers

larger red
combs on
Ad. males

Heavily feathered
feet

base colour
varies dep.
on light
Ochre in
overcast
light

glossy
sienna

DGRobertson

Left
RED GROUSE SKETCHES,
GLEN ESK
Derek Robertson
Watercolour

INTRODUCTION

IT IS A MAGICAL TIME, that period before the grouse arrive, when one can lean against the front of the butt, elbows resting on the damp heather, and look out over the vista ahead. For a sportsman it is the moment of appreciation and anticipation. Appreciation of the vast effort in time, money and emotion, by owner and keeper alike, that precedes a day on the moor and anticipation of the thrill to come.

In this book the artists try to reflect those emotions. The thrill of seeing a pair of grouse with a full brood of chicks in early June will conjure up feelings in those involved in moorland management that only a painting can reflect. Mere words are insufficient to describe the excitement of a covey of a grouse flying towards the butt, the artist, however, can portray that moment in a way that raises the heartbeat of the sportsman and creates an empathy between them.

Although predominantly concerned with red grouse, this book also covers the other members of the grouse family, capercaillie, ptarmigan and black grouse. It is not meant to be a comprehensive study of the habits and habitat of this unique bird, rather an insight into how each artist approaches his subject and a rich tapestry of images that reflect their passion for grouse.

THERE ARE FEW more unusual sights in the uplands than the black grouse lek, where the males fan out their lyre-shaped tails, drop their wings, puff out their neck feathers and strut. They start before dawn when all you can see in the murky light is the puffball of white feathers on their bottoms and hear the cooing noise, similar to that heard in a dovecote. It is a remarkable sight, all the more so because they do this for months on end. There is a brief lull in late summer and autumn whilst they are moulting and so not looking their best.

For the rest of the year, irrespective of the weather, or the presence of the grey hen – the female black grouse – the males will gather at the lek site and pose in vain splendour, engaging in occasional mock fights though never serious enough to damage their feathers! In spring, the hens attend the lek regularly in search of the dominant males with whom they will mate. That service fulfilled, the males will play no further role in the breeding process, preferring to continue with their vain display. The lek site measures around an acre in size and is divided up into small territories, with the dominant males holding the areas closer to the centre.

Black grouse are generally found at lower altitudes than red grouse, preferring moorland edges and open forests, but they will frequently overlap. They have suffered a catastrophic crash in population in the last two decades, dropping from 25,000 to around 6,000. Much of this is due to habitat loss and predation, with the result that many moorland owners, in an attempt to halt the decline, will no longer allow them to be shot.

Their habitat of choice is often young plantations but they will move on once the overhead cover becomes dense. Clearings in mature forests that allow the regeneration of birch scrub are also popular, and research is being carried out to assess the value of this type of habitat in an attempt to stem the decline.

Left and opposite
GROUSE STUDIES
Owen Williams
Pencil

THE BLACK GROUSE
At a glance

SCIENTIFIC NAME	*Tetrao tetrix*
CLASSIFICATION	*Resident*
LENGTH	*40cm to 55cm*
WINGSPAN	*65cm to 80cm*
WEIGHT	*Male 1.3 kg Female 1 kg*
LIFESPAN	*Around 8 years*
POPULATION	*Around 6,500*
NUMBER OF EGGS	*6 to 10*
INCUBATION	*25 to 27 days*
HABITAT	*Moorland edges and open forests. Generally at a lower altitude than red grouse*
DIET	*Buds, birch shoots, pine*
COLLECTIVE NOUN	*Covey*
SHOOTING SEASON	*20th August to 10th December*

THE RED GROUSE
At a glance

SCIENTIFIC NAME	*Lagopus lagopus scoticus*
CLASSIFICATION	*Resident*
LENGTH	*37 to 42cm*
WINGSPAN	*56cm to 63cm*
WEIGHT	*550g to 690g*
LIFESPAN	*Up to 10 years*
POPULATION	*250,000 pairs*
NUMBER OF EGGS	*6 to 10*
INCUBATION	*22 days*
HABITAT	*Heather Moorland*
DIET	*Mainly heather but also seeds, berries, insects*
COLLECTIVE NOUN	*Covey*
SHOOTING SEASON	*12th August to 10th December England, Scotland and Wales*
	12th August to 30th November Northern Ireland

I T IS OUR ONLY truly wild resident gamebird; that is perhaps why the red grouse excites so much passion. Unlike most other gamebirds that can be reared and released, its survival is closely linked to the management of its habitat; the heather moorland. It is a subspecies of the willow grouse that can be found across the northern latitudes of Europe, Asia and North America. Unlike its close relative, however, it has a diet almost exclusively of heather, which is why habitat plays such a pivotal role in its success.

THE CREATION OF MOORLAND

When standing in a grouse butt it is hard to believe that the surrounding landscape is largely a result of man's influence. These are some of the wildest parts of Britain, yet what we are trying to preserve today is largely our creation, albeit accidental. Up until 5,000 years ago most of the areas of moorland we know today were covered in trees and the small grouse population that existed would have lived on the edges of woodland above the tree line and in small clearings. From Neolithic times through to the Iron Age trees were cleared to make way for crops and livestock. Because moorland is always wet plants do not rot, instead they accumulate and, as they compress, form a layer of peat over the soil. The minerals in the soil are washed away by the high rainfall and those plants, such as heather and cotton grass, which tolerate a poor soil, flourish.

Prior to the rise in popularity of grouse shooting the management of heather moorland was carried out by shepherds. They burnt the old heather to provide fresh shoots for their sheep to graze on. Ironically this provided the ideal habitat for grouse which prefer older taller heather in which to hide from predators and new fresh growth upon which to feed.

HABITAT

Habitat management is now carried out for the benefit of grouse and heather burning is one of the most important aspects of this. The objects of burning are to provide a mixed habitat for grouse containing patches of different aged heather. Older heather provides areas for nesting and concealment. Freshly burnt areas are used for sunning and dusting whilst the younger heather provides food for the grouse. The nutritional content of younger heather has more nitrogen, phosphorus and potassium and is therefore superior to older plants.

A Brief Natural History

Red grouse are essentially a territorial bird and towards the end of October the cock birds will begin to re-establish their territory. The most sought after areas contain a diversity of habitat, such as patches of different aged heather, other edible vegetation, and water. The size of the territory will be between two and thirty acres depending on the quality of the habitat. He will display by flying steeply into the air and making a series of loud barking 'aa' calls, and then descend, with rapidly beating wings, neck extended, tail fanned, and a slowing 'ka ka ka' call.

During harsh weather the grouse will abandon their territories and congregate in large packs in search of food. As the weather becomes milder they will disperse and territories will resume. The grouse will often pair up at this time, sometimes resuming the pair bond from the previous year, and the male will defend his territory vigorously.

The time between pair bonding and egg laying is critical for the hen grouse, as she must build up her reserves at the end of a hard winter to enable her to survive incubating the eggs. This period coincides with the emergence of buds on the cotton grass which provides a highly nutritious source of protein and the hen will consume all she can.

The hen usually builds her nest in thick heather on the edge of a burnt patch, affording her cover as well as visibility. It will be sited reasonably close to grit and an area where the chicks can feed and water. A slight hollow is scraped out and lined with heather and grass in which the hen will lay a clutch of between six and ten eggs from late April to early May. After around twenty-two days of incubation the eggs will hatch and it is at this time that weather is critical. Warm weather is ideal during hatching, though intermittent rain is necessary to produce the insect life upon which the young grouse will feed for the first few weeks of their life. The cock grouse will take an active part in the process, defending the hen during incubation and being in attendance when the chicks go out in search of food. Should anything happen to the hen he will even take over raising the brood.

Young grouse grow rapidly, being able to fly at two weeks old and are fully grown at just over a month. It is during this period that they are at their most vulnerable to harsh weather. Heavy snow, rain, or frost can all occur on the moor during early summer and if this occurs before the chicks are fully grown but are too large for the parents to brood and protect them high mortality will result.

The diet of the young grouse will begin to change after about three weeks and contain more and more heather.

Left
RED GROUSE
Terence Lambert
Medium

To help them extract the nutrients from this fibrous diet they collect grit in their gizzard which helps grind down the heather before it enters the intestine. During the brief summer other plant species will supplement their diet as they build up their strength for the harsh winter ahead.

The family group will remain together well into the autumn, forming the coveys that fly through the line of butts on the glorious twelfth. It does not take long for these coveys to start merging into large packs, several hundred in size in good years, all the while becoming wilder and more wary.

Grouse Disease

Should the grouse survive the vagaries of weather and predation two other factors can cause their demise. The first is the strongyle worm and the second louping ill. Volumes have been written about grouse disease and what follows is just a very brief outline

The strongyle worm is a tiny parasitic nematode which burrows into the wall of the blind gut of the grouse. This is where the grouse absorbs the nutrients from the heather after it has been broken down in the gizzard. The worm causes internal bleeding and reduces the digestive efficiency of the grouse. Once the numbers present in the blind gut start to exceed 5,000 the grouse will become weaker and, as numbers increase, will die. The worm spreads by laying eggs, which pass out of the grouse in their droppings. The eggs develop within the droppings and moult twice before becoming infective larvae. These climb up the heather plant and wait to be eaten by a grouse where they will make their way to the blind gut and develop into adults. And so

the cycle repeats. During years when grouse numbers are high the worm will spread rapidly which normally results in a crash in the population.

The other major disease that grouse suffer from is louping ill which is spread by ticks, a small relative of the spider family that lives on a diet of blood sucked from the host. Louping ill is a virus that attacks the central nervous system causing the sufferer to stagger or 'loup' eventually being unable to walk. It can prove fatal in ten to sixty per cent of sheep and eighty per cent of grouse. It is spread by the tick's saliva moving from tick to host and from host to tick.

Ageing Grouse

From a grouse management point of view old grouse do not breed as well as young ones. More importantly, they also carry a larger quantity of the strongyle worm and so will increase the worm burden on the moor, thus infecting the younger, healthier grouse. So it is better to shoot the older grouse during the season to improve the health of the moor.

The proportion of old to young grouse will also give an indication of how well the breeding season has gone. In the game larder there are several methods of assessing the age of a grouse. The most common is to look at the primary feathers of the bird: in a young bird, early in the season, the third primary will be slightly shorter than the second.

Above
BIRD TO PICK
Owen Williams
Watercolour

A ROUGH TRANSLATION of the Latin name *Lagopus mutus* is hairy footed and silent. A delightful name for a rarely seen member of the grouse family. Few, but the most dedicated sportsmen and hill walkers, will venture into their harsh domain and trying to spot the birds, with their near perfect camouflage, takes a practised eye. The most difficult time to see them is when there is a light covering of snow with bare rocks – then all one can hope is that their movement will give them away.

Like the mountain hare they change their colouring in winter becoming pure white, except for their dark bill and tail feathers. The males are distinguishable from the females at this time by a small black streak running from the bill to the eye. Ptarmigan go through three plumage changes during the year. As the snow begins to clear they change to their spring plumage from late February to early May. From June to September they will have a complete moult renewing their wing and tail feathers and taking on a delicate grey plumage. From September to November it will revert to its winter plumage.

Normally found at an altitude of around 3,000ft they are the only birds inhabiting these inhospitable surroundings all year round. In very harsh weather they will seek shelter in rocky corries.

Although the territories of the ptarmigan and red grouse rarely overlap, their diet is very similar, relying on heather, blueberry and crowberry for their nutrition. However, the former will resort to anything that can provide sustenance, even pecking the lichen on rocks.

Right and top
PTARMIGAN STUDIES
Owen Williams
Pencil/watercolour

PTARMIGAN
At a glance

SCIENTIFIC NAME	*Lagopus mutus millaisi*
CLASSIFICATION	*Resident*
LENGTH	*34cm to 36cm*
WINGSPAN	*54cm to 60cm*
WEIGHT	*400 to 600g*
LIFESPAN	*Unknown*
POPULATION	*10,000 pairs*
NUMBER OF EGGS	*5 to 9*
INCUBATION	*21 to 26 days*
HABITAT	*Scottish mountains at around 3,000ft altitude. The only bird inhabiting these inhospitable surroundings all year round*
DIET	*Heather, blueberry and crowberry*
COLLECTIVE NOUN	*Covey*
SHOOTING SEASON	*12th August to 10th December*

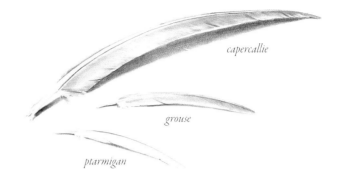

capercaillie

grouse

ptarmigan

THEY ARE HUGE, as big as a turkey, and a male approaching in full display is an impressive sight, and one to be wary of, for they will attack intruders into their territory. As their favoured habitat is natural pine forest, as opposed to plantations, they will rarely be seen in open moorland. Their population is estimated to be around 3,500 of which only 1,000 are female. There is a danger of a repeat of what happened in the 1700s when they became extinct in the British isles. The main cause of this decline was a combination of deforestation, a succession of poor breeding seasons, and a mini ice age. Although shooting would have contributed to its demise it was not a significant factor and it was sportsmen who imported a few birds from Sweden in the early 1800s and successfully re-introduced them in Perthshire.

They are now found only north of the River Forth and predator control and habitat preservation are the best methods to preserve this impressive member of the grouse family.

Top
FEATHER COMPARISON
Owen Williams
Watercolour

Right
CAPERCAILLIE STUDY
Jonathan Sainsbury
Watercolour

CAPERCAILLIE
At a glance

SCIENTIFIC NAME	*Tetrao urogallus*
CLASSIFICATION	*Resident*
LENGTH	*60 to 87cm*
WINGSPAN	*87cm to 125cm*
WEIGHT	*Male up to 5 kg* *Female up to 2.5 kg*
LIFESPAN	*Around 8 years*
POPULATION	*Around 3,500 of which only 1,000 are female*
NUMBER OF EGGS	*7 to 11*
INCUBATION	*24 to 26 days*
HABITAT	*Mature pine forests in Scotland with an undergrowth of heather, blaeberry and crowberry*
DIET	*Pine needles and buds but will also eat seeds and berries*
COLLECTIVE NOUN	*Tok*
SHOOTING SEASON	*No longer on the quarry list*

K.J. Sykes.

KEITH SYKES

B E IT WILDFOWLING, pigeon shooting, rough shooting, partridge or pheasant shooting you will invariably be presented with the regular array of retrievers and spaniels as part of 'the team'. The formal shoots have well-established, traditional working patterns: the Labradors and other retrievers such as Goldens and Flatcoats being placed in anticipation behind the guns, whilst the springers, cockers and those illegitimate 'sprockers' are busy hunting in the beating line in order to flush the birds.

In contrast however, the demands of grouse shooting and the management of the grouse moor give rise to the addition of more specialised breeds, many of which are not native to the British Isles. The spaniels and retrievers still have a role to play but this too can be said for pointers, setters and various 'Hunt, Point, Retrieve' (HPR) breeds especially when the birds are 'walked-up' and not driven. I am fortunate in that from the east window of my coastal studio I gaze onto the 12,500-acre grouse moors of the Abbeystead Estate, albeit seven miles in the distance and not to mention the windmills. The

Estate, which is near to the city of Lancaster and the Trough of Bowland is currently owned by the Duke of Westminster who purchases it in 1981. Abbeystead still boasts the world record for the number of grouse shot in a single day. This was achieved on 12 August 1915 when a team of eight guns shot 2,929 birds.

Each grouse moor is different and requires appropriate management based on experience and knowledge. In the early 1980s Meryl Asbury, in conjunction with keeper Steve Orzechowski, began the grouse counts with English Pointers on the Littledale beat of Abbeystead. Whilst this exercise provides valuable statistics on bird numbers it is also a valuable training opportunity for the dogs and their handlers. The theory is that a number of set square kilometres of ground are worked and the grouse on those areas counted twice a year, and as the years pass and more data is collated the trends become more apparent. Both favourable and less favourable areas for the grouse are surveyed to enable a realistic estimate of the resident population for the whole moor to be established.

For an intensive two week period in the month of March, Meryl and her husband, Peter Asbury, work their team of setters and English Pointers across many of the grouse moors of North Lancashire and parts of Yorkshire, undertaking the 'spring count' of breeding pairs. Thirty to forty breeding pairs in a set kilometre would give the keeper cause for optimism but as they will all tell you, the weather can have a major influence on the breeding success and potential disaster is never far away.

For a few weekends in April and at the end of August the Asburys' dogs are worked closer to home on the arable land of the Southwest Lancashire Plain surveying the numbers of grey partridges.

In July the couple return with the dogs to the grouse moors to count the broods. The numbers of adult and young birds on the same kilometre patches of ground are counted. A healthy return would be a ratio of four young to one old bird. These statistics give the keeper a fair indication as to how successful the breeding season has been and consequently an idea as to how many birds can be harvested come the shooting season. The counting begins as early as 6 am during periods of hot weather with the intention of completing the task before midday specifically for the benefit of the dogs. A number of either English Pointers or the setters – possibly two, three or four – are taken from the dog trailer. One or sometimes two dogs of the same breed work concurrently with the others following behind on leads with another handler. They

work for approximately ten minutes before being replaced in rotation. As and when a dog goes 'on point' and the grouse are subsequently flushed the birds are counted and the numbers recorded.

The English Pointers and Irish Red Setters are totally different in both style and appearance but the end result is the same, whether being used to count grouse or to shoot over the dog is cast off and when it winds a bird it goes 'on point'. When shooting is taking place the guns would wait until they approach the dog 'on point' before loading the guns. They pass the dog and walk slightly ahead of it as it moves slowly towards the hidden bird, then as shooting etiquette dictates, the guns will shoot their respective birds as they flush. Retrievers would then be deployed to pick the fallen birds. Unlike the English Pointers trained and worked in the United Kingdom, in Europe and the USA English Pointers are also trained to retrieve the shot birds.

Whilst the English Pointer dates back hundreds of years some minor dog breeds such as the Langhaar (German Longhaired Pointer) were introduced as recently as 1993 to the United Kingdom. Many of the long established HPR breeds from Germany that now appear on British grouse moors were originally bred for all types of hunting including deer and wild boar, consequently they are often tall, fast and strong. From my observations I can see there

Right
IRISH RED SETTER 'ON POINT'
Scraperboard

is a high degree of skill in working and training these dogs and the use of the wind is paramount to success. The breed of dog used on the grouse moor varies considerably but each has its own specialist use.

The ongoing threats from foxes, weasels, stoats and corvids are similar year by year and

Right
LATE AFTERNOON SUN
Scraperboard

need to be addressed accordingly and ideally before the grouse begin to nest. When the sheep are taken from the moor in winter the keeper has the opportunity to set his snares. Foxes are renowned for following sheep tracks and where these narrow can provide the ideal site for a snare. It is often during the January moon that the dogs and vixens can be heard barking as a prelude to mating. A reasonable snow fall allows for tracking and gives a good indication where fox is to be found. This can be in holes or rocks on or adjacent to the moor. Without such precautions foxes are able to stray from the surrounding land to take the easy pickings of nesting birds or vulnerable young grouse.

As an artist I am inspired by the movement, speed, agility and style of the dogs bred especially for work on the grouse moors – they are a joy to watch and I find the flowing coats of the Irish Red Setters particularly enchanting. I strive to capture the loyal expression of the faithful Labrador delivering a bird to hand or the mischievous expression of a workaholic spaniel. It has often been said that one Labrador is the same as the next but from my personal observations their facial features and expressions are as individual as our own.

Left
GERMAN LONGHAIRED POINTER
Scraperboard

Below
ENGLISH POINTER
Scraperboard

K.J. SYKES

SIMON GUDGEON

IN ANSWER TO the question 'For two days' labour, you ask two hundred guineas?' the artist James McNeill Whistler replied 'No, I ask that for the knowledge of a lifetime.'

Few people have any concept of how long a piece of art takes to complete or what goes into its creation, yet the creative process is, for me, the most fascinating aspect of sculpture. Once a piece is completed I feel a combination of elation, exhaustion and depression; elation from the fact that I have completed what I set out to achieve; exhaustion from long hours and single-minded dedication; and depression because it is now finished.

The sculptures in this chapter were completed in 2006 though all of them were started long before then. A wildlife sculptor has to spend time studying his subject in its environment before venturing into the studio. This initial process is one of the most important aspects in the creation of a work of art. Through knowledge the artist develops an understanding of the creature that he hopes to represent. Unless one understands and appreciates one's subject there is no passion and trying to create a thing of beauty without passion is futile.

The red grouse fascinates me as an artist, sportsman and conservationist. Over the years I have drawn, painted, sculpted, and even written a book about them. Each visit to a moor, though, still fires me with enthusiasm and inspires me to return to my studio and once again tackle this alluring subject. There is, however, a period of time between the inspiration and the creation which can stretch out for weeks, months and sometimes years. It is during this time that the idea for the sculpture is refined, dilemmas resolved, and, for me, one of the most important aspects, the design of the mount or base upon which the sculpture will rest.

As an artist, watching a covey of grouse coming towards the butts is truly inspirational. I see movement, shape and form and those are the building blocks for the sculpture. Following inspiration comes research. One must understand how they fly. Knowledge of wing movement, muscle structure and skeletal

form are gained by spending time watching them in flight, photographing them, studying dead grouse – measuring and dissecting them.

The initial inspiration and research is probably the easiest part of the whole process, it can be done to a time limit and is not mentally taxing. The next stage is much more difficult. Sculptures or paintings depicting the natural world should be works of art in their own right irrespective of the subject matter. They should be more than a mere depiction or representation of a bird or animal. Even if the viewer has no empathy with a particular subject they should be able to appreciate the piece of art before them. The composition, dynamics, movement and form all contribute to the success of the work. Sculpture should be dynamic. Even though it is a static piece of metal or stone it should generate a feeling of movement and the viewer's eyes should flow over the piece.

Sketches, or quick sculptures using clay or wax can resolve some of these elements. Most of the time, though, I visualise the piece in my head during quiet moments, building it again and again in my mind's eye. Every time I come across something that does not seem right or jars I go back and start the process again. At any time I have innumerable ideas swirling around up there; some can be resolved in a matter of days, other can take years. The *Covey of Flying Grouse* is an example of the latter.

The idea first emerged whilst I was researching for the book *A Passion for Grouse*. I had sculpted a three-quarter life-size single flying grouse and a pair of flying grouse but was inspired to create a life-size covey. The issues to resolve were how many grouse to include, how to mount the birds and what wing beats to use. The first was not difficult; it has to be an odd number to give it balance and seven would make the sculpture too

large and three too small. The latter issues though took nearly six years to resolve.

Sometimes inspiration can come from the most unlikely sources and whilst watching a World War II film I was captivated by the image of a Spitfire doing a barrel roll. From that image came the idea of sculpting one bird as it flicks over to change direction, essentially having a grouse doing a barrel roll. Although a covey of grouse consists of a group of birds, which will, at any one time, have their wings at various stages of flight, the upbeat, downbeat or occasionally

gliding, this would, as a sculpture, have the propensity to look messy. I felt that a repetitive image of a bird changing direction would give the piece a flow and movement.

The next issue to resolve was how to mount the birds in this position. For me the mount is one of the most important parts of a sculpture. It is intrinsic to the whole piece and is what will give it movement and flow. Sometimes the mount is designed to accommodate a particular pose, although often the design of the mount will come first and then I will spend time thinking of the ideal bird or mammal for it.

Sculptures of flying birds pose a unique problem as one is trying to give the illusion of flight, of a bird that has broken its bond with the ground and is soaring in the sky. Yet with a sculpture the bird has to be supported so an illusion of space needs to be created to give the impression that the bird is not attached to its mount. The initial idea for the *Covey of Flying Grouse* was to make a mount that had the whole sculpture resting on a horizontal plane such as a table or sideboard. This, however, would not allow enough space for the five grouse to go through their full range of movement, which is when the idea of a wall mount began to develop.

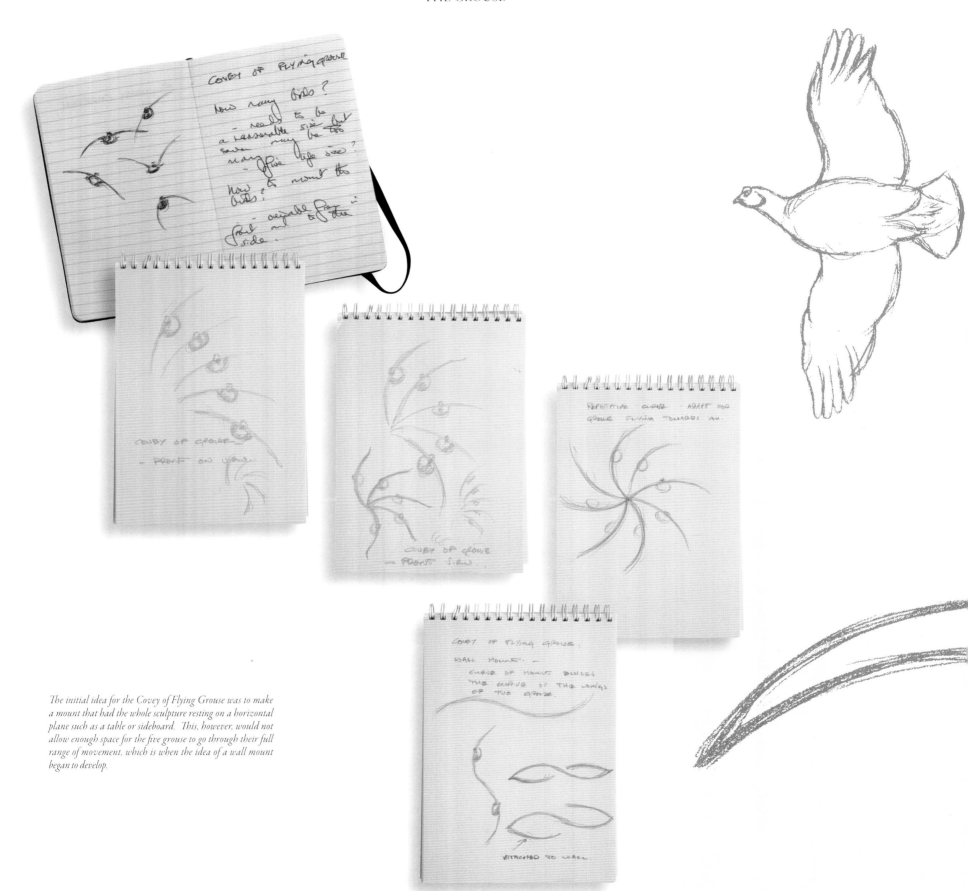

The initial idea for the Covey of Flying Grouse was to make a mount that had the whole sculpture resting on a horizontal plane such as a table or sideboard. This, however, would not allow enough space for the five grouse to go through their full range of movement, which is when the idea of a wall mount began to develop.

The moment when all the dilemmas have been resolved is hugely exciting and that is the time to get into the studio and make a start. Complicated sculptures like the *Covey of Flying Grouse* have to be made in several parts and it is not until all those pieces have been cast that the whole thing can be assembled. Just to give you an idea, the covey involves casting twenty-four separate pieces. This is a nerve-wracking time because up until that moment one is never totally sure that the idea is going to bear up to reality. Years have been spent developing the idea, weeks have been spent in the studio fabricating the piece, thousands of pounds have been spent casting it and then the day arrives when it is time to put it all together and see if it works as a sculpture.

The *Covey of Flying Grouse* is a piece that from concept to reality took many years and during that period there was no pressure to complete it to a time schedule. I could let the idea slowly develop until I felt ready to start it. This is one of the reasons I do not do commissions, for the luxury of working on a sculpture over a long period means that no corners have to be cut, no dilemmas left unresolved, and the final sculpture will be a piece that I am happy to put my name to.

WALL MOUNT

COVEY OF FLYING GROUSE
LIFE SIZE, WALL MOUNTED.

SIMON GUDGEON

Right
COVEY OF FLYING GROUSE *(Side view)*

Above
FLYING GROUSE
Plaster relief

Below
COVEY OF GROUSE
Bronze, Limited Edition of 12
19cm high, 52cm wide and 36cm deep

This sculpture explores the dynamics of a number of birds forming a family group. Some are resting, some preening but there is always one on alert, looking out for danger, ready to warn the rest of the covey of an approaching predator.

Unlike many of my sculptures, where the base is an important and integral part of the piece, the covey has no base. Instead the base is whatever surface they are placed upon, be it a table or a sideboard, enabling them to integrate with their surroundings.

Below
PAIR OF GROUSE
Bronze, Limited Edition of 12
22cm high, 30cm wide and 22cm deep

This piece explores the dynamics of grouse after they have pair bonded. He is alert, semi-displaying with tail flared and eyebrows raised, ready to repel any invasion onto his territory.

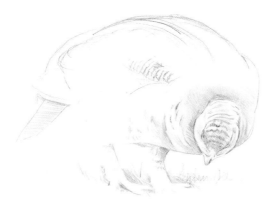

Opposite
COCK GROUSE HEAD STUDY
Oil on paper

Left
FEEDING GROUSE
Pencil

Below
CALLING GROUSE
Oil sketch

BEN HOSKYNS

I SAW MY FIRST grouse on the morning of 16 August 1976. I had been invited to tag along with my father for a week's shooting over setters at Balnacoil Lodge on the Brora. I hadn't a clue how lucky I was; I had only been shooting for two years and I assumed that this was the way it would always be.

My Game Book reveals that I had connected with some thirty-odd 'things' with my 4.10 up until that point – rabbits, pigeons, pheasants and a very unlucky jack snipe (legal in those days) – and I managed to point it in the right direction at a grouse, eventually, on the last flush of that first day.

The two setters, Rose and Rory, had worked superbly all day and had given me several earlier chances to no avail. We were only a couple of hundred yards from where we had parked the vehicles when Rose stopped and set and was shortly backed up by Rory. A single cock grouse flushed, giving me a crossing shot. Most of

my game shooting up to that point had been walked up and, with such a little gun, I had learned to be quick off the mark. My first grouse fell dead into the heather but I had also learned not to be too quick to claim – that someone else may have fired, too. They hadn't but I had to wait until the second half of the barren pair had also fallen before being congratulated.

It was a magical week in that long hot summer. We walked for many miles, diving into the burns to slake our thirst whenever we could and 'miraculously' cresting a rise to find the pony with our piece just when we thought we could walk no further. We didn't shoot very many – thirty-five brace for the week – but I have never forgotten it or the magical essence of a grouse moor.

I managed to add another grouse to my total of seven the following year in Perthshire when a friend's family took a cottage out on the moors for a week. We were dogless and consequently didn't get too many chances. We had a few hundred acres of hill with odd patches of heather and one or two coveys of grouse to ourselves and we walked all day for an occasional sighting and infrequent shot or two. I had no idea that it would be more than twenty years before I had the opportunity to swing a gun on a grouse moor again and I can remember in my twenties wondering whether I ever would.

It was only when I began to paint for a living that I had the opportunities to really study grouse and their habitat although I had absorbed as much as I could when stalking in Perthshire in the eighties. The more I painted them, the more fascinated I became with them and when I was asked to paint specific moors I would find myself amongst people who really knew their grouse and they would spend the rest of the day answering my endless questions whilst we searched for the right spot to paint.

I have spent more time on Knarsdale than any other moor, having been commissioned to do a series of paintings of each of the beats for Mark Osborne and I fell deeply in love with the area as I got to know it.

The story of Knarsdale's (including the Asholme beats to the east) remarkable turnaround is a fascinating one and shows what can be done when the commitment is there even when a moor is thought to be 'beyond redemption'. This fifteen thousand acre moor with five and a half days' driving had an all-time annual bag record of 3375½ brace shot in 1936. When Mark took on the lease, in 1991, the ten-year annual average bag was a little over 750 brace. A team of American guns took some of the early shooting in that first season. After the second

drive on their first day, the bag stood at a brace and a half of grouse and three snipe. They ended the day with 17½ brace and the three snipe. And that to double guns.

In 1997, after seven seasons and a considerable amount of work from a dedicated team of exceptional keepers, Knarsdale produced a new season record of 5052 brace. In 2001, only four seasons later (and after a big crash in 1999) the record was broken yet again with 5292½ brace shot. And that with a third of the moor closed down for over a month in August and September due to the Foot and Mouth crisis. They were lucky to shoot at all when many moors were unable to do so but one wonders what the bag would have been had they not been restricted. It is thought that Knarsdale will one day produce, maybe, seven thousand brace in a season, given the right conditions.

In complete contrast, there is a little moor of some seven hundred acres opposite Knarsdale, above the eastern banks of the South Tyne. Williamston stands out amongst the Knarsdale and Asholme hills which appear to be largely 'white' although the heather is there or the grouse wouldn't be. An oasis of heather-clad hillside that can be seen pretty much as you leave Alston, Williamston has been in the Gill family for nearly three hundred years.

In 2002 I did a painting of High Beat on Knarsdale for my Game Fair exhibition at Broadlands. Neville Gill wandered on to my stand and recognised the view and I soon found myself painting what he and his ancestors had been looking at for three hundred years. It is often the way with grouse moor commissions: you paint a view of the neighbour's ground.

With little grazing pressure, good keepering by Albert Ridley and a handy buffer zone of well-keepered ground around it, Williamston has had some remarkable bags. Neville has game books going back to 1911 which show a ninety-four-year average of 137 brace. However, the all-time record day of 146½ brace, made on 12 August 1957, is unlikely to be broken. It transpires that the keeper and his son got up at 5.30 that morning and went and blanked in the bog next door! The Gills ended that season with 352½ brace.

Above
RUFFLED FEATHERS
Oil on paper

The hen is every bit as beautiful as the cock.

Left
SKETCH FOR RUFFLED FEATHERS
Pencil

Above
GROUSE OVER SHEEP
Oil on paper

Right
GROUSE OVER SHEEP
Sepia

One of several studies for the oil.

When it comes to work, I can think of more trying things to do than to sit amongst the heather listening to the grouse and looking at some of the country's most spectacular views. During the course of the year, I get to see some very beautiful places but grouse moors are always a source of enormous inspiration, perhaps because we do not have them on our doorstep here in Suffolk. The colours can change so much from day to day – the richness of the heather, even in winter; the vivid greens of the mosses and the meadows on the moorland edge; steep gills blanketed with bracken; the blue-greens of the rushes and the yellows of the humps of bilberry. A shaft of light on a distant hill or the shifting shadows, from clouds, that are a feature of long uninterrupted views would allow one to paint the same view over and over again without any feeling of repetition. And yet, there is a feeling of time standing still amongst these hills – that nothing much has changed in a hundred years or more. Drive off the hill and head for home and there is a sense of leaving behind something extraordinary as you exit the grouse moor bubble.

Whether shooting or painting, the drive North is usually spent worrying about the weather. It is a long way to go to find that it is foggy. Whilst this is an inconvenience when doing commissions, it can be highly dangerous when shooting as the beating line can become fragmented so that some beaters may almost be on top of the butts when the first horn blows.

I have frequently had to wait for things to improve when I am on a working trip and once, when I could only see fifty yards, had to come back later in the week. But things can change just as quickly from bad to good so it is often worth hanging on. I have sometimes sat for five hours or more in my truck, buffeted by the wind and rain, high up on a moorland track waiting for a break in the clouds. And you can drive across neighbouring ground through ever-thickening fog to find it is completely clear on the moor you are going to paint. Ultimately, although it is always preferable to see the moor in good light, all I really need is the shape of the hill and I should be able to add the light.

Without a doubt, the foulest shooting weather I have experienced was on a mid-September day on Snake moors in Derbyshire. It was my first double-gun day and I had a friend loading for me. He said he thought he was going to die.

I cannot stand wearing leggings and accept that when it is raining, I will get damp. It was cold and blowing hard but I hadn't realised that it was quite so wet. As I turned from my butt after the last drive before lunch and took my first step towards the lunch hut, I saw water spill out from the top of my boots! It was a tremendously exciting day with fast and furious grouse but it was as much as you could do to focus on the horizon in front and a lot of the wonder of grouse moors – the calling of grouse and the sights and sounds of other wildlife – was lost in the rawness of the day.

Much of the enjoyment of any day's shooting is about the other wildlife you see and hear but you can easily be caught napping which could lead to a certain

amount of trouble. There is often a long wait before the first grouse appear and, naturally, you look around, noticing a pipit or a wheatear on a rock in front of you. You hear a curlew calling and search the vast skies for its familiar shape. A swallow passes and you idly watch as it flits by. Out of the corner of your eye, a bee drones over the swathes of heather, only you suddenly realise that it is a single grouse, on set wings, hurtling towards you. The gun comes up automatically and the bird falls into the heather beside your butt. As it drops below the skyline it ceases to be a silhouette and you realise that you have just killed your first blackcock complete with £500 fine attached. It is lovely to see blackgame but it is nicer still to get a side view when they are flying over someone else!

****

Grouse are one of the most delightful birds to paint with their rich and immensely varied plumage, both in colour and markings, and I never tire of looking at and painting them. They make rather good models, too – obligingly sitting atop a dry-stone wall as you drive past or gritting by the roadside so you can draw to a halt twenty yards away, sit back and observe.

In flight they are, quite simply, breathtaking to watch. Few birds come close to their speed and agility – and agility at that speed, especially for a bird the size and weight of a grouse, is astonishing. They have enormous stamina, too. I have seen a large covey of a hundred or so come the best part of a mile, pitch in seventy yards in front of the guns only to flush immediately and go the whole way back, over the beaters and out of the drive!

I have nothing but respect for their remarkable hardiness and ability to survive in what can be, in winter, a pretty hostile environment. But it is this magical environment that makes seeing grouse such a wonderful experience. I would always rather be somewhere beautiful, whether I am watching or shooting, and few places come as beautiful as a grouse moor.

Above
SKETCH FOR ONE OF THE WILDLIFE
HABITAT TRUST PAINTINGS
Pencil

Left
FLYING GROUSE – FOR THE
WILDLIFE HABITAT TRUST
Watercolour

Opposite
AFTERNOON SUN
Oil on canvas

I liked the idea of the track keeping the grouse 'in bounds' and that the end of the covey is drawn back in, as if on elastic. This could be part of an enormous pack.

Right
DISTRACTION
Oil on canvas

...idly watching as a swallow flits by.

Below
FLYING GROUSE STUDIES
Pencil

I never tire of painting grouse in flight.

Left
OVER THE MOORS
Oil on canvas

Right and Below
FLYING GROUSE
Oil on paper

Ben Hoskyns

Opposite
GROUSE BUTT
Oil on paper

I have never actually seen a grouse perched on a butt but I have seen enough droppings on them to know that they regularly do so.

Above
FLYING GROUSE
Oil on paper

Left
HEAD STUDIES
Sepia

Right
INITIAL SKETCH FOR THE
2006 WILDLIFE HABITAT TRUST
CONSERVATION STAMP
Pencil

A great honour to be asked to paint the stamp and a huge delight that the subject was red grouse.

Left
COCK GROUSE
Sepia

Below left
BLACKCOCK SKETCHES - ALSTON MOOR
2004
Pencil

Below right
GROUSE SKETCH
Pencil

Above
PREENING GROUSE
Pencil

_____

I love the shapes preening birds make.

Below
BLACKCOCK
Oil sketch

TERENCE LAMBERT

ANY WILDLIFE SPORTING artist striving for originality, when tackling the grouse family has an almost impossible task. No other species has been painted so often. Thorburn, Harrison etc were such prolific painters, showing grouse in every posture imaginable. They created a visual language of their own. A Thorburn grouse dust bathing, or a covey, with his trademark short stiff wings were bound to influence those that followed. Harrison's heather moorland with big water colour skyscapes have become iconic, leading purchasers of contempory sporting art to expect that image. Some of my contempories have enough talent that they have tackled the subject without obvious signs of being derivative. Their genius is possibly displayed in this book, but why should I further their careers by naming them! It is no accident that the collective noun for a gathering of wildlife artists is a 'bitch'.

To understand why we artists approach the subject the way we do, it helps to look at the apprenticeship, our personal history as artists. I have spent much of my working life as an illustrator. With an ability to paint in fine detail, much of my work has been dedicated to studying the natural world in macro. An illustration by its nature should be easy to interpret, but what has always driven me is that the subject should have its own history. It should exist outside of the rectangle, not just any red grouse, but a living breathing individual.

So where to start? With a lifelong passion for the natural world the data base is already stacked with impressions and memories, some of which are documented in sketch books and records of previous works. It is very important never to presume to know the bird, landscape or branch about to be painted. I always look afresh at the subject in question and bring all the props into the studio. I am fortunate to have a collection of cabinet specimens of a large number of birds, these allow me to measure and study feather colour and pattern (*pluckings*) without having to resort to using photographs. After the question, 'how long has a particular painting taken to paint?', the second is, 'do I use photographs?' Painting in fine detail, it is reasonable to presume the source for the work would be the camera. Simply replicating from a photograph, however skilled the artist, always disappoints. As a reminder of a landscape or detail of a bird it is acceptable, but copying an entire pose and arrangement from a photograph says nothing about the artist's unique eye and mind.

How the light is treated in a composition is vital. Light in a painting conveys time and place and is the catalyst for a successful work. Working directly from nature in the field is the best way to get it right, but that never seems possible with the pressure of work. Perhaps when the imperative of earning a living from the craft is resolved that frustration will be eased.

Living in the hills of central Wales we still have the remnants of what once was a very productive grouse moor within walking distance of the house. The red grouse are still occasionally flushed, but the heather moor is much reduced by the planting of softwoods back in the 80s. The small population of black grouse was stable when the trees were young, but gradually diminished and by the end of the 90s disappeared. After a long hike in the hills in '98, the melancholy bubbling of a lone cock bird drew my attention to a magnificent old bird with full lire tail and glowing red comb. I gave him posterity by painting *The old campaigner.* He was probably the last bird on the moor! The red grouse can still be found in small numbers, and appears to be a paler form than his northern cousin, *Strutting his stuff.*

I had to return to a very old sketch book to find any reference to the most elusive of the grouse, *Caledonian showers* and *Ptarmigan Cairngorms.* At best, a sketch book is a personal diary. This drawing took me back to a beat on the river Findhorn during a summer shower when I chanced upon a cock capercaillie high in a Scots pine. I was used to only seeing this monster grouse strutting his stuff during the lek, or the fleeting view of birds flushed. It remains one of my favourite sketch book drawings.

Having pored over bird books when a child, I viewed grouse as exotic. They lived in habitats so far removed from the Surrey countryside. The Hog's Back, east of Farnham, was my mountain, and it was there, with pockets full of slow worms and knees permanently scabbed, I fell in love with the natural world. Ptarmigan grew in my child's mind to be birds the size of pheasants. Their eggs were like gems

to me. I desired them as a celeb covets diamonds (*Eggs*). Seeing the birds for the first time against the grandeur of the Cairngorms, I was amazed at just how small they are, and marvel that they manage to survive the hostile winters in the Highlands

I never feel I have finished with an idea until I have revisited using a different medium or atmosphere. Examples being *The old campaigner* and *Frosty Lek*. I feel I learn so much more about the whole creative process by working with different pigments. A traditional illustrator's medium, ink on scraper board is a great favourite of mine (*Covey*) The ink is applied with a brush on a surface of china clay. Fine marks are achieved by scratching the surface with a fine point, I prefer a scalpel blade. The medium requires patience, good eyesight and an abstemious lifestyle. Fortunately that eliminates ninety-nine per cent of my fellow artists! Working with different medium has always challenged and excited me, but banished to a desert island I would hope the tide would wash up a pile of pencils and a waterproof pack of handmade paper. It would be some time before I attempted to build a raft.

Above
EGGS
Watercolour

Left
GROUSE PLUCKINGS
Watercolour

Above
THE OLD CAMPAIGNER
Chroma colour on canvas

Above
COVEY
Ink on scraper board

Left
FROSTY LEK
Chroma colour on linen

Below
BLACK GROUSE STUDIES
Pencil

Left
PTARMIGAN, CAIRNGORMS
Chroma colour on canvas

Below
STRUTTING HIS STUFF
Chroma colour on linen

Above
CAPERCAILLIE
Chroma colour on canvas

Right
FLIGHT STUDIES
Pencil

Opposite
GROUSE ON A BANK
Oil

Below
BRACE OF GROUSE
Watercolour

RODGER McPHAIL

I HAVE GOOD REASON to love the red grouse. Not only has this splendid game bird supplied me with superb sport and excellent dinners, it has, over the last thirty years, provided a considerable percentage of my income.

The reason that *Lagopus scoticus* has been so financially rewarding is that grouse shooting is a rich man's sport and rich men can afford the luxury of original paintings.

It is true that you can shoot grouse on a limited budget. Walked up grouse can be had for a reasonable price, and wonderful sport it is too, but driven grouse are horribly expensive. Several factors add to the cost. Pheasants, partridges, ducks and geese can be found all over the world – red grouse are found only in the British Isles, and in tiny, fragile regions of the British Isles at that. Other game birds can be reared in large numbers to supply the demand for sport – not so the grouse.

Most moors have years, sometimes several years together, when grouse numbers are too low to permit shooting. Through these lean times a keeper's wages must still be paid. On the big day itself a whole army of beaters, loaders, flankers, dog men and caterers add to the expense. It's the Rolls-Royce of field sports, the champagne and caviar of shooting! To stand in a stone butt gazing out over the heather is, therefore, a great privilege, especially to an artist who could only be there as the result of the generosity of clients and friends.

I shot my first grouse thirty years ago on Eggleston Moor in County Durham. I had been commissioned to paint moors before that, but this was the first time I had been invited to bring a gun and stand at the end of the line for a few drives. I'll never forget the heart-thudding excitement of seeing the first birds skimming low towards the butt and the elation when, after several shots, one finally crumpled into the heather in a burst of feathers. That excitement has never palled to this day. For exhilarating sport and magnificent surroundings there is simply nothing to beat it. Downwind grouse make a testing target even for the experts, and for a mediocre shot like myself, they can be downright humiliating!

Most sportsmen only see grouse at the beginning of the season, but for the artist it is interesting, indeed essential, to see them at other times of the year. I love to watch them in spring when the males are performing their territorial display flights, and in the early summer when they are tending their young families. They are excellent parents, brave and selfless in protecting their young. In the bleak mid-winter the moors can be dark and lonely places, but the grouse are then in their best plumage. At the end of winter, heather burning, though seldom seen by the shooters, is a very paintable subject. If you walk over the moors you are unlikely to see them until they fly, so the best way to observe grouse is from a vehicle.

Whenever I watch grouse I feel a great sense of affection and pride for this most British of birds. Let unsmiling pedants bleat that it is merely a regional variation of the willow grouse – this is *our* bird, as British as Yorkshire pudding and, to me, symbolises everything that is good about the sport, wildlife and scenery of our islands.

The bird itself is so admirable in appearance and demeanour. The dark, modest plumage is offset by the white feathery feet like spats and the scarlet wattle is the perfect finishing touch, like a red carnation in a buttonhole!

It is fitting that such a fine creature should live in such a splendid habitat, the wild, sprawling heather moorlands of Scotland and the north of England. Indeed, a great part of the pleasure of grouse shooting comes from spending a day in such a wonderful environment. It is small wonder

that it has been painted countless times over the last century or so by generations of artists. The fact that the sport has been depicted in oils and watercolours so many times causes a problem for the artist. How can you add something new? Luckily, there is such a variety of weather conditions in Britain that there is an endless choice of light effects, atmospheres and moods to choose from.

The typical grouse flight pattern is a few seconds of rapid wing beats followed by a long glide on stiff, downturned wings. The gliding part of the flight is relatively problem free. Victorian painters, without the benefit of high-speed photography, painted *all* the birds in this position, reminiscent of those old racing pictures with all the horses frozen in that strange rocking-horse stance.

It is the flapping part of the flight that causes a dilemma. I have taken hundreds of photographs of flying grouse, and the camera usually catches the wings in positions that the eye doesn't see. The wing beats are just a blur to the naked eye or, in good light, the wings are seen in two positions – at the top and bottom of the stroke with a blur in between. This, however, is a very difficult thing to paint convincingly! I usually opt for a compromise between the impression the eye gives and the truth the camera reveals.

A young grouse simply and lightly roasted is a real treat, especially when cooked by my wife! The flesh delicately flavoured by its heathery diet. My own preference is to eat them as fresh as possible. Grouse tend to be shot in warmer weather than most game and they can go off very quickly if hung.

Plucking and dressing birds for the table is a good discipline for an artist. It familiarises you with the way the joints work and how the feather tracts fall. It is also interesting to see how much individual variation there is in the plumage, even among birds from the same moor.

Our famous grouse is a bird to be proud of. It is fascinating to watch, challenging to paint and delicious to eat. As a sporting bird there is no other to match it. It has been called the king of game birds, a title I think it richly deserves.

Above
HEATHER BURNING
Oil

Right
RISING GROUSE
Oil

Above
WEARDALE
Oil

Left
GROUSE AND STAG
Oil

Left
GROUSE ON THE MOORS
Oil

Below
FLYING GROUSE
Watercolour

Above
DRIVEN GROUSE
Oil

Right
THREE BLACK COCKS
Oil

JONATHAN SAINSBURY

I WAS EIGHT YEARS OLD and lying on my back in the hay, when a black bird with a lyre-shaped tail flew across the sky. I ran back to the house and looking through my bird books was convinced I had seen a black grouse. This was unlikely as home was Warwickshire and the closest black grouse in the 1950s would have been Wales or Cannock Chase.

I suspect I saw a melanistic pheasant with a damaged tail or a misplaced cockerel. But at that age my imagination was greater than my ability to be objective. After all, I spent much of my time dressed as a Pterodactyl flying, (falling) from the garage roof or persuading my friends to go on 'safari'. Often I went alone. They wanted to play football, but I couldn't understand what all that was about. However, that experience in the hay brought to my attention that grouse existed.

Red grouse, black grouse, ptarmigan, capercaillie – little did I know as a youngster what a large part of my life would be given to making pictures of them. I now live in Scotland and the trials and tribulations of these birds is a constant fascination. They are vulnerable and not adaptable. Each lives in a particular and precious environment, which limits its ability to flourish, but for me as an artist, their dramatic and ever-changing landscapes, powered by the turning of the seasons, makes for wonderful pictures.

In the nineteen eighties I would travel north to Scotland from my Warwickshire home. It was vital to source the needed information for making pictures with the most efficient use of time. Speyside, therefore, was an important stop, because all four kinds of grouse could be found with the least amount of travelling, depending on weather and good luck.

The red grouse at first sight appears like a brown Christmas pudding of a bird, set in a tweedy brown and ochre landscape, but on closer inspection the landscape is a myriad of colour made up of mosses, lichens and wildflowers and likewise, the grouse is not just brown, but an intricate patterning of black, various umbers, ochres, siennas and white, all brought to life by the vibrant crimson wattle glowing like neon on a grey day in spring. Close

inspection of the grouse is necessary to see this handsome plumage, therefore specimens for study must be found. Dead birds can sometimes be found on the roads around Tomintoul but if unsuccessful with roadside kill, a local butcher/game dealer will often supply feathered birds. So, armed with illustrative information, the next task would be to draw live birds in the wild. Again, the road to and from Tomintoul would give easy access to birds and allow me to make quick pencil sketches to capture the gesture and shapes they make, looking from the heather.

I then need information about the world they live in to feel confident before starting a picture. So after drawing the birds I would next sketch pieces of landscape and collect mosses, lichens, plants and rocks to inform myself about that micro landscape amongst the heather.

In winter, daylight is short, so all this flora and fauna had to be taken to my hotel room to be worked on in the darker mornings and evenings. It was important for me to find a place to stay that asked no questions as I dragged half a mountain top through the lobby.

In many a Highland hotel a stuffed capercaillie can be found. It is there to taunt you. Take a good look, for it will probably be the only one you will see. Looking for capercaillie in the field is an impossible job. Walking for hours through Caledonian pine forest brings no results.

Far left
MOUNTAIN HARE
Tempera gesso and oil

The tempera mixed technique allows a detailed building of fur on the creature and lichens and vegetation in the landscape.

Left
PINE MARTEN AND CAPERCAILLIE
Charcoal and watercolour

This picture was inspired by a wonderful picture by Bruno Liljefors in which a pine marten is pulling a caper from the top of a tree.

Clockwise from right
RED SQUIRRELS
CROSSBILLS
WREN
CRESTED TIT
Charcoal and watercolour

Best then to forget the quest and enjoy the forest. At first glance, the forest seems very still and lifeless. Yet if you sit down and wait, your hearing will tune to the subtle noises and gradually it comes to life. You will more often hear the red squirrel – its claws scuffling on the bark of the pine – before you see it. You will hear the crack of a twig as a roe deer moves. Crossbills and crested tits will pass by, as will the delightful and ever-present chaffinch and wren. And if you are lucky, you will just spot a capercaillie vanishing into the distance, having left its well-placed bough in an ancient Scots Pine, from where it has been watching you for some time.

In desperation, and needing a drawing of this 'B52' of the bird world, whose head is said to be like a donkey, I have drawn them in captivity at Kingussie in the Highland Wildlife Park. It makes the job much easier. And in spring, the male will happily display and the females are there in their glorious russet plumage to be studied, too.

My first sighting of a Capercaillie in the wild was in the Abernethy forest – as it is recorded in the painting *The Sentinel*. What a wonderful moment that was. Sadly, sightings have been seldom repeated.

On my travels, capercaillie and grouse could be found in Speyside, as could ptarmigan, if I took the ski lift in

Aviemore up to the top of the Cairngorm. That terrain, however, is not my favourite and I preferred to travel west to the road that leads from Kishorn to Applecross. The road hairpins its way to the very summit of Sgurr a Chaorachain, where the landscape is fantastic, with views from Wester Ross across to Skye. Even more of a bonus was that the birds could be found within moments of leaving the car.

The weather can be wonderfully unpredictable. I remember one February day, when I drove in gale force winds to the summit, where the wind had moulded the snow into slipstream shapes behind projecting rocks. Not wanting my car door to be ripped off by the wind, I turned into the wind and got out. I was blown right over. Struggling into the lea of some escarpment or rocky ridge, I sat down, relieved to be out of the freezing blast. Looking to either side of me were ptarmigan, who were there with the same idea. I drew them for a little while, but

having to take my gloves off to draw, my hands froze, so instead I studied them. Then we all watched the weather, which was reminiscent of H.G. Wells' *Time Machine* – clouds racing overhead, with moments of snow, mist and sunshine all happening at lightning speed.

On other trips in spring I have found this pretty bird in the warming sunshine, the male in his new Spring plumage, making his rather unattractive, guttural call, contrasting with the plaintive note of the newly-arrived golden plover.

Ptarmigan moult three times a year, making them able to vanish before your eye if they stop moving: white against the snow, and mottled grey and white against the rocky outcrop, they are perfectly camouflaged for the changing seasons. If I want specimens to draw, Perth Museum has a good quantity of skins from all seasons and one phone call will result in specimens being laid out for my inspection – long live libraries and museums!

The ptarmigan is a tame bird which helps it become invisible. Often I have been looking for them, peering into the distance, only to find them standing around my feet, especially in autumn, when the family group is young and unworldly. This pretty bird is worthy of our respect. It lives on a meagre diet in extremely hostile conditions.

Twenty-four years ago I first travelled to Glen Artney, having been told I could find black grouse there. Sure enough, there they were, posing in the birch trees, looking exactly like the Thorburn pictures I had previously studied. I now live two miles from this glen and see black grouse frequently. The males, with their black plumage and lyre-shaped tails, look very exotic. To watch them lekking is to spy a great ritual of which most people are unaware.

When Kate and I were unmarried, I tried to impress her. Early one morning, having just driven up to Perthshire overnight from Devon, I pulled into a lay-by just feet away from a lek I had found the previous year. Ten yards away from us, the black grouse performed their magical dancing and warbling, before breaking away to feed on a new larch plantation nearby. Likewise, having demonstrated to Kate what a first-rate man I was, we went our way to a Highland breakfast.

Left
RED GROUSE, ROCK AND HEATHER
Charcoal and watercolour

Using a square format makes for a circular composition of this
cock and hen grouse.

Above
RED GROUSE IN SUMMER
Charcoal and watercolour

By not painting the distant landscape, I hoped to convey the
richness of colour and pattern in the micro-landscape.

Above
MRS BOUCHER'S GROUSE
Watercolour and charcoal

Charcoal allows me to abstract the scene and stops too much detail

Right
RED GROUSE TAKING WATER
Watercolour

Red grouse drinking in the early morning of a new day. The mist obscures the view and the imagined sound of water hopefully concentrates the eye on this restful scene.

Left
GROUSE OVER THE BURN
Watercolour and charcoal

At first the moor looks flat, but it doesn't take long until something of interest comes to the viewer's attention.

Left
GROUSE, WALL AND SUMMER FLOWERS
Tempera, gesso and oil

Using alternate layers of tempera and oil glazes made this picture come to life, especially the wall and grouse against the softer distance.

Above
GROUSE AT ARDVORLICH
Tempera and oil

Winter makes for dramatic scenery and the layering of tempera and oil helps build up the snow and emphasises the turbulent weather.

Right
GROUSE OVER THE MOOR
Sepia watercolour

Working with sepia allows ideas for pictures to be worked quickly, without the confusion of colours.

Right
BLACKGROUSE AT THE LEK
Charcoal and watercolour

Below
MANSFIELD'S BLACKGROUSE
Tempera and oil

The dominance of the blackgrouse within the picture cannot be overpowered by any amount of colour, as this painting shows.

Above
INVERSNAID
Oil

The title is taken from a poem by Gerard Manley Hopkins.
The painting portrays elements of the poem and I share in the
sentiments of the last verse:

What would the world be, once bereft
Of wet and of wildness? Let them be left,
O let them be left, wildness and wet;
 Long live the weeds and the wilderness yet.

Left
BLACK GROUSE FLYING
THROUGH THE BIRCHES
Watercolour

Below
THE OLD ROWAN TREE
Watercolour

Above
SNOWY LIMITS
Watercolour and charcoal

I love this picture. The charcoal lends itself to this display of camouflage, two birds easily visible, but a third appearing out of the rocks only after closer inspection.

Right
THE SENTINEL
Oil

My first sighting of a Capercaillie in the Caledonian pine forest was just like this.

Opposite
STORM GROUSE
Watercolour

Left and Below
GROUSE STUDIES
Pencil

OWEN WILLIAMS

MY HOME HERE in Cardiganshire is within shotfall of a small piece of moorland, a place I used to roam with a gun as a youngster after snipe, hare and duck. Had I been born a generation or so earlier I would have had the chance to shoot grouse over that same ground. Sadly, over-grazing has taken its toll on the heather over the years and the last time I saw any evidence of grouse was a solitary pile of droppings seen on a walk about twenty years ago. Today Cardiganshire, and indeed much of Wales, has precious few grouse. Unlike many areas of Scotland and Northern England where there is a concerted regime of moorland management over wide areas, Wales has a patchwork of moorland where the lack of commercially viable sport has resulted in a failure to invest in effective management and thus brought about the sad decline of this fascinating bird.

My first recollection of grouse was at the age of eleven, not here in Wales, but whilst on a family holiday to visit my grandmother who at the time lived in Allendale, Northumberland. Travelling in an old Land Rover from Aberystwyth, my two brothers and I sat in the back in far from comfortable conditions. We made the long and cold journey north with the occasional stop to stretch legs. One such stop was on a high moor north-east of Brough where, next to the road ran a burn containing sandstone boulders. As I strolled down this burn I noticed that the rocks were rich in fossils. At the same moment a grouse flushed a few yards away and with an irate 'get back, get back' call flew off across the moor.

How often must it happen that a person comes to a significant crossroads in their life without knowing it. Looking back now I realise that on this moor I had been at a crossroads. The fossils in the burn were the first I had ever seen, the notion of those bivalves living in a shallow Permian sea some 250 million years ago captivated me, as fossils do for many youngsters, and kindled an interest in geology which would steer my school studies away from art. With hindsight I now see that it would have been better to have taken more notice of the grouse, which I now paint for a living, rather than the fossils. Eventually my path towards a career as a geologist was blocked by my repeated failure to achieve the B grade in Chemistry 'A' level that would have secured a place to study geology at University.

Today, after a detour through the world of advertising which dried the wet behind my ears, gave me a commercial grounding and enabled me to find my wife, Sally, I am one of those fortunate few who make a living from their art. In recent years I have been lucky enough to be treated to shooting and fishing in the UK and further afield by collectors of my pictures, without whose great generosity I would lack the inspiration for so many of my pictures.

It is only very recently that I have had the chance to shoot grouse. Before this I occasionally walked grouse moors as a beater or picking up which gave me the opportunity to see grouse. This season for the first time I had the spectacular experience of standing in a butt on one of the finest moors in England shooting driven grouse... I now see what all the fuss is about. There is a point of debate that comes from those who don't shoot that we would get as much excitement using a camera rather than a gun. My experience shooting driven grouse confirms my view that for me there is no substitute for the tingle of excitement we get as hunters when we near that heightened moment of pulling the trigger. As sporting artists our work is to get that sense of excitement into our paintings.

Gradually over the past twenty years I have come to the realisation that I am a landscape artist, for it is not

Above and Opposite
GROUSE STUDIES
Pencil

just the bird that interests me but that fantastic moment in time that the shooter experiences when he is about his sport. As important as the bird, is that feeling of time and place that is conveyed by the light in the sky and the quality of colour and contrast it places on the landscape. A good illustration of this is seen in my recently completed painting *Argyll Grouse*.

My first sporting picture was painted at the age of thirteen after an experience flighting teal on a pond near my home. I had become inspired by books and articles on shooting. I yearned for that great landmark moment of shooting my first duck. To this end I fashioned a crude decoy out of a polystyrene block, which I painted in acrylic paint to look something like a teal drake and set out in failing light to my flight pond. The night was crisp with the remnants of a recent snowfall still lying in frosted patches between the rushes. The clear sky promised a sharp frost, my stage was set, and with the unnaturally bobbing decoy sitting out on the water I waited.

Looking back, the pond was never fed and the chance of a teal calling in was remote, but I was full of youthful optimism. Eventually, after a short wait I heard that air-tearing sound of an incoming teal, looking over my hide of rushes I could make out a single teal on the pond next to my decoy. With pounding heart I rose to my feet and flushed the teal, which obligingly flew low against the glow of the last colours of the rich sunset. I hastily shouldered the gun and then forgot the safety catch, a trick I have managed to repeat a few times since. Feeling stupid at my tensing against a

non-existent recoil, but relieved no one was watching, I realised that I had missed a great chance.

On reflection it didn't matter that I hadn't shot the teal because on that December evening in 1969 I had experienced the three major ingredients that today feature in my paintings – wilderness, atmosphere and hunting – and that's what inspired me to start painting.

In the years since, as a self-taught artist, I have worked, and often struggled, to develop the skills with which to convey my passion for such moments through my pictures. I no longer have the picture that I first drew on my return home that evening. Years in a portfolio in a damp loft saw it decay and it was eventually thrown away along with countless sketches of ducks and geese that were drawn through my teen years. I would like to think that despite an obvious lack of technical skill, it conveyed the excitement of that moment I was trying to capture.

A great debate has raged in recent years about what true art is. Many in the contemporary art world would look upon sporting art as being too figurative and commercial to be taken as serious art. I think that they are wrong, many sporting pictures demonstrate a great level of skill in the chosen medium and beyond this convey enormous passion for the subject. This they hold in common with some of the finest paintings by great masters such as Michelangelo, Van Gogh or Turner. Of course there has always been a tendency for art to push the boundaries and stimulate controversy, but surely it also has a role to play in the pure celebration of a thing of beauty as exemplified by Constable's *The Hay Wain* or Rodin's *The Kiss*.

The greatest compliment I have been paid by buyers of my work is whilst looking at one of my imagined landscapes, and knowing that it was of nowhere in particular, they have said, 'I have been there' meaning emotionally they have an affinity with the painting.

Being a self taught artist has meant that I have had to bumble my way towards developing my technique and this has been a long process of trial and error. I have several books on watercolour technique on the shelves in my studio. Probably to my detriment I have not studied them too much. It is probably irrational, but I don't want to be tutored too much by any one exponent for fear of my work becoming too much like theirs.

Those of us who paint in watercolour suffer the added difficulty of not being able to correct mistakes as we go. It is easier when you can paint over the mistake in a medium such as oils. It sometimes happens that a picture will end up in my waste bin when the realisation comes that all is not well, quite often when many long hours have been spent in its execution, others by some inexplicable process, seem to flow easily from palette to paper.

The depiction of flying birds is not easy, the reality is that wings are usually seen as a blur and rarely in any detail, so all artists have developed their own a sort of caricature. It is interesting to note how Thorburn's drawing of flying grouse changed over the years with stubby wings in his early pictures to better proportioned in his later work. As a teenager I spent long hours copying from published works of Thorburn, J.C. Harrison and McPhail, this along with observation made in the field helping to gain a better understanding of form.

The mental process here is that with constant observation and practice the brain builds a three-dimensional model of the subject. Despite it being depicted in two dimensions the brain develops and refines an understanding of what is going on in the part of the model that it out of sight. Over time it becomes possible to sketch a bird flying from a variety of angles and elevations from scratch, the process takes many years but it is important to keep refining with continuous sketching. My biggest regret is that with the pressure keeping up with the demand for my work, I spend too little time making field sketches. Each time I paint a new grouse painting I will redraw the birds trying

Right
GROUSE DOWN
THE TRACK
Watercolour

to change angles and elevation to create a realistically pleasing covey: this is a good discipline as it stops you repeating past mistakes. Painting a large covey, I draw the individual grouse on pieces of tracing paper and try to arrange them in a convincing pattern over the background. The mind has an annoying tendency to arrange things with an element of symmetry, which can result in a covey looking very contrived. Observation is very important whilst out in the field – I find this a good excuse for my poor shooting due to making detailed mental notes on birds flying by.

On a recent trip to shoot grouse in Northumberland I was struck by how low the coveys flew past on a particularly windy day, observations like these are invaluable in getting realism into a picture.

Light is an essential ingredient in any painting, setting the mood for the picture and taking you right into the scene. Beyond conveying a feeling of place it can give clues as to the time of day and the weather at the time and thus adds to the narrative. I have always been fascinated by weather and often bore friends and family pointing out particular cloud formations or flashes of sunlight on landscape. On recent trips to South Africa I was struck by the different quality of the light there. Sitting painting at our hunting lodge in the Karoo, it took me a while to decipher the different range of colours and values I was trying to capture in my first African watercolour. Unlike in most of Europe, African light has high contrast and the shadows are usually very strong and warm in nature.

The first thing I do when I start a painting is to decide on the light, both the direction of lighting on the scene and the quality of light. This dictates the colours I will use on the first washes of the landscape, warm colour for summer scenes and the colder blues for winter. All my pictures start with the sky with an initial watercolour wash to shape clouds and sky. This involves using several colours working them in whilst the paper is still wet, there is little time to fiddle about as the paint dries very quickly and once done can look very messy if reworked. I have a large collection of sky reference photographs in my studio that help get the ball rolling at the initial stages of a painting. I try not to copy these photographs too loyally, which is difficult anyway when dealing with large areas of watercolour washes. If the picture is not a specific commission where I have to get the detail of a particular landscape I can then start filling in where I want to place some of the key elements of landscape such as distant hills, a burn or peat hag.

If the birds are to be large elements in the picture I have to take care to leave areas of white paper into which these can be painted so that any areas of white on the bird can be depicted by the white of the paper. Over-painting with white paint is an option, but there is nothing brighter in a watercolour painting than pure white paper and white

Above
BOWES COVEY
Watercolour

Left
GROUSE STUDY
Pencil

paint can look very dull in comparison. Sometimes if the grouse are to be seen against a sky then I can lift off a small amount of wash to get back to plain paper again, or use masking fluid to cover the desired area. After a wash has been applied this is rubbed off to expose the white paper beneath.

My drawing of the grouse is usually done as a line drawing on a sheet of tracing paper and this faint outline is then transferred to the watercolour paper. Sometimes I will do several preliminary sketches in a sketchbook. With these I will try and get highlights and shadows onto the birds that tie in with the light direction in the painting. This is done using a soft 3B pencil and a rubbing stick or fingers. Eventually when I am happy with the placing of the birds in the composition I will start painting in the watercolour detail.

Had I have gone to art college I know my tutors would have insisted on a far more disciplined approach to building my pictures but this is the process I have worked out for myself over the years and for the most part it seems to succeed. Watercolour is not an exact medium, at times there is almost an element of alchemy about it, which I like. It does mean that at times my litter bin is full of

wasted watercolour paper and my family have to suffer my frustration induced moods but this is occasionally counterbalanced with my state of euphoria when it all comes right. I have a long held passion for watercolour and a great admiration for artists such as Russell Flint, Edward Seago and the many fantastic Victorian exponents who managed the medium so well.

As I mentioned earlier, my experience of grouse has been limited and it has only been in recent years on numerous forays to Scotland that I have more opportunity to study them.

In my early years as a sporting artist I was commissioned by a client to paint a picture of ptarmigan on an estate in Invernesshire called Garrygualach. Located on the south shore of Loch Garry, access was limited to a landing craft that was phoned for on your arrival at the nearby Invergarry hotel. The accommodation was basic but the food was good and there was a real feeling of being 'away from it all'. Behind the lodge the ground rises up into the high mountains where the ptarmigam live.

Each day I accompanied the guns along with guides Peter Isaacson and Ken Aldridge to look for ptarmigan on mountains with exotic names such as Carn Dhu and

Scurr Chonnich, where the flora is alpine, covering the areas between scree and boulder with a varity of mosses and lichens. The perspective at this height is dominated by being nearer to cloud base than the glens and lochs below.

My first sight of ptarmigan was of a small flock walking across the rocky ground ahead of the line of guns. They appeared quite docile and I began wondering whether this was the worthy sporting quarry it was made out to be. Once they flushed it was instantly apparent what a testing bird this was. With an explosive flush they were airborne and away in no time, demonstrating an uncanny ability to curl into the nearest corrie giving the guns little time to shoot. To see a flock of twenty birds fly away onto the next hill with the white of their wings glowing against a backdrop of a shadowed corrie is an awe-inspiring sight, the stunning landscape adding to the drama of the moment. Those three autumn days walking in the mountains above Loch Garry gave me a fascination for the Scottish Highlands and in turn inspired me to put a greater element of landscape into my pictures.

A few years ago I was invited by the owner of an estate on Deeside to paint some small pictures for his game book. One windy morning whilst walking on the summit of the highest mountain on the estate I was puzzled by a group of ptarmigan that on seeing me started to move in my direction. I was sitting upwind of them and as they got nearer I realised that in order to take off they had to be out of the downdraft behind the slope they were on and so they had to walk into the wind towards me. For a while I wondered whether to get my sketchbook out or the camera, in the event they took off and were away before I had a chance to do either.

One of the most spectacular settings for a line of grouse butts must be on the Invercauld estate near Glenshee. I was planning for an exhibition that I was due to have at the Nigel Stacy-Marks gallery in Perth in 1999 and was keen to get some ideas for local landscapes. I contacted the keeper on the estate and asked if I might be able to get up onto the hill. At first he was somewhat reluctant as on the

Above
GROUSE STUDY
Pencil

Left
AUGUST SHOWERS
Oil on canvas

only day I was in the area the owners were shooting and understandably he didn't want to have an itinerant artist roaming about. I suggested that I would be happy to walk with the beaters and he agreed. The day was dull with drizzle and there was hill fog on the tops, as I drove up the hill with the keeper it looked doubtful that there would be much shooting done. On the first drive I was placed as flanker near the end of the line of butts, with the mist coming and going the nearest gun thoughtfully placed his stick as a marker to avoid shooting in my direction. There then ensued a long wait whilst the beaters brought in the surrounding hillside. The moment when grouse came through the fog past me was very dramatic and is featured in my painting *The Flanker's View*.

Over the years as I have met some fine keepers and moor owners and it has become apparent that the running of a successful grouse moor requires huge understanding and dedication from owner and keeper alike. The variables that dictate the success or otherwise of a moor are many and complex for this is a wild bird which offers supreme sport. As a sporting artist, to have been allowed an insight into this fascinating world is a privilege and leaves me in little wonder that the grouse has featured so prominently throughout our history of sporting art.

Left
ARGYLL GROUSE
Watercolour

Above
COVEY DOWN THE GLEN
Watercolour

Right
GROUSE OVER THE HAGS
Watercolour

Left
GROUSE STUDIES
Pencil

Right
PTARMIGAN STUDY
Watercolour

Left top
DISTANT SUNLIGHT
Watercolour

Left bottom
PTARMIGAN GROUND
Pencil

Below
BURN GROUSE
Watercolour

Left
WINTER GROUSE
Watercolour

Right
GROUSE STUDY
Pencil

Below
INVERCAULD,
THE FLANKER'S VIEW
Watercolour

Above
PTARMIGAN OUTCROP
Watercolour

Left
WINTER PTARMIGAN
Watercolour

Right
PTARMIGAN STUDY
Watercolour

Opposite
PTARMIGAN LIGHT
Watercolour

Left
ABOVE LOCH ARKAIG
Watercolour

Below
PTARMIGAN STUDY
Pencil

Opposite
LEKKING BLACKCOCK STUDY
Watercolour

Left
WORKING SKETCH
Pencil

ASHLEY BOON

IT IS A GLORIOUS September morning. In the valley where we live the heather has turned, the rowan berries are bright and the colours of autumn are creeping across the hillsides. I'm outside our small house getting my five year-old daughter onto the school bus when suddenly from the hill comes that sound 'Owk-owk-owk-ok-ok-k-k-k-k-k-okk, go back, go back, go back, go back-back-back-back-back-back'. And I can't help myself. I simply have to stop whatever I'm doing to scan the hillside for that compact, neat, dark form. And there he is, stretched up to his full height, proudly defending his patch, and again, that challenging call 'Go back, go back, go back-back-back-back-back-back', a red grouse. Yet again I am thrilled to be standing outside the house where I now live looking at one of our most special birds, and silently I thank whatever providence has brought me the good fortune to be living in this beautiful valley with such special neighbours.

When I was a young boy some kind friend, knowing of my interest in wildlife and wildlife art, gave me as a Christmas present a reproduction portfolio of old prints of upland birds. Ring ouzel, merlin, wheatear and so on, and of course grouse, both red and black. I never thought as I pinned them to my bedroom wall that I would find myself waking each morning to look out on their wild habitat, but here I am, 750 feet up in the Cumbrian fells surrounded by heather moors and 'in-by ground' or hill pasture.

The red grouse has to be the most sporting bird Britain has to offer. To stand in a butt on a moor, eagerly watching for the swirling covey that will be on you and past in the blink of an eye, is one of the most thrilling experiences I have enjoyed, and on the many fortunate days I have spent walking up, I am always amazed by the speed that a crouching grouse can take wing and be away so fast.

I grew up in Northamptonshire, a long way from the moors, and like so many others who live in the tamer reaches of our island, I used to count the days to the annual August trip in pursuit of our most native of game birds. I used to drive up to Caithness with my best mate Steve, worrying every mile about the grouse prospects, and the many long days walking the moors in his company make up some of my most special sporting memories.

My first trip to Caithness (my first real encounter with red grouse) was a few weeks after I had graduated

Left to right
BRIGHT EYE RING, RED WATTLE & NEAT WHITE MOUSTACHE
COCK GROUSE STUDY
DRIVEN GROUSE STUDY
GROUSE PORTRAITS
Watercolour

from art college. I had no money and no prospects, but I couldn't have cared less! I have seldom felt more excited than when I took my place in line to walk up for the first time. Every detail is as fresh today as was that dry bright morning. The awkwardness of the borrowed 12 bore, the heather, the rocks, the jolly spaniels, and then at the top end a handful of dark shapes burst forwards in front of the line. A few soft 'pop pops' from the farthest guns and one of the shapes folded back into the heather, to be retrieved, the first grouse of the day. It had all seemed so slow, much slower than when a little later, on hissing wings, a covey rose nearly at my feet. All I had to show was a bruised shoulder. But how I ran to gather my prize when I did connect, and how carefully I held that first grouse to examine him in detail. The bright white-eye ring, neat beak, the intricate markings, his stiff primaries and dark tail and those wonderfully feathered legs and feet. It wasn't until I moved to Cumbria nearly twenty years ago that I got the opportunity to get to know these birds better.

Since then I have enjoyed many days on the moors, sometimes lucky enough to be in a butt, more often walking and also on rare occasions hunting them with falcons. One of the most memorable grouse I ever shot was with my good friend David Ogilvie, over one of his English Setters, with a one hundred and fifty year old black powder muzzleloader! The Labrador retrieved it, but afterwards someone questioned whether or not I'd shot it or if it had hit a rock and died in all the smoke!

Can there can be any other British sporting bird whose general perception has been so coloured by its depiction in so many Victorian sporting scenes? The image of the driven covey speeding on fixed wings invariably captioned something along the lines of 'T'wards the Butts' or 'Afore the Butts' is in itself almost a definition of cliché. Yes, they do look dynamic as they skim on down-curved wings, but it's pretty obvious they must flap at some stage or we'd be able to gather the crashed ones from the heather at will! It only struck me when I spent time in the beating line quite how mobile they are. To watch a plump grouse as it creeps through the heather, it seems a very un-athletic bird, but

as those of you who have waited in the butts know, this isn't true. I watched one old cock grouse in particular as I was beating one day and he was actually looking over his shoulder in full flight! They twist and turn, stretch and flex; a far cry from what a contemporary of mine perusing yet another 'O'er the Guns' type piece described as, 'Christmas puddings with M's on'!

My own approach to painting a driven covey is to start with some very basic sketches. What I'm trying to do is capture the feeling of a grouse in flight. I work with a black pen on layout paper, so I can throw away sheets that don't work immediately. When I feel I have got a few shapes that work, I put them onto tracing sheets and rearrange the images over and over again, until I have a

pattern I'm happy with. I will even cut out the shapes in black paper and arrange them upside down, so that I can concentrate on the composition rather than the fact that they're grouse.

I don't know why people expect artists to be on a different emotional level, but they often do. Years ago I did a painting for an exhibition showing the butts from behind. In the distance were the butts, guns and grouse skimming through. In the foreground I painted a dead grouse lying in the heather. The morning after the private view, the exhibition opened to the public, and I must admit that I was rather hungover. A lady stood in front of this piece and said 'I can feel your sorrow and I feel the sadness and pathos you're trying to express, isn't that right?' She left in a huff after I said 'No, just a good day's grouse shooting!'

Left
WORKING SKETCH
Pencil

Above
DRIVEN GROUSE SKETCH
Pencil

Ashley. R. Boon

Despite the thrill of grouse flying towards you, or their sudden appearance as if catapulted from the heather, I am drawn to showing the more private side of their life, producing pieces that are just enjoying the birds themselves. I like to draw and paint on tinted paper, which allows me to work in positive and negative, building an image quite quickly. For want of a better way of describing them I call them 'studies'. I also enjoy observing the other part of their season when the grouse turn their thoughts to reproduction. Instead of the shy bird hiding in the heather he becomes a different creature. Strutting and aggressive he looks splendid with his wattles up full and red. On a still morning I love to stand in our garden and hear the challenging calls and watch territorial chases and display flights from my studio. They look especially striking in a frost or snow.

Having the chance to observe these birds often I can tell those few wiseacres I meet from time to time at the Game Fair or other exhibitions, who helpfully point out that I have got the colouring wrong, that there is virtually no such thing as a typically marked grouse! Take the time to examine a bag of grouse in detail and you will see that the colour variation is infinite. The underwing coverts alone vary from almost pristine white to almost entirely dark. Having said that, I'm always drawn to specimens with a bright eye ring, red wattle and neat white moustache.

~Capercaillie and Ptarmigan~

Of the four species of grouse we have in Great Britain the most difficult to see are the capercaillie and the ptarmigan. My experiences of these two species have been all too brief, but notable nonetheless.

I made up a shooting party to go after ptarmigan near Dalwhinnie years ago. We did get a few in the bag, and I have two of the birds I shot set up. They are very beautiful birds, pursued in even wilder country than red grouse. I have not seen them often, but I always look out for them when stalking in high country, alerted to their presence by that creaking call. They are quite hard to see on the ground, but as they flush it is as if the stones have taken flight. It is an extra treat on a day's stalking to surprise a covey of ptarmigan and watch them sail away on those clean white wings.

The capercaillie was, for a young birdwatcher growing up in the Midlands, a bird of almost mythical status. So it was a wonderful and exciting opportunity when I was invited to help count displaying capercaillies at a secret location in Strath Spey one early spring a few years ago. This counting consisted of going out into real Caledonian forest the evening before and setting up hides on the lek, then leaving our beds at three in the morning to trek through the snowy dark to sit huddled in the cold to see what appeared at first light. The first morning I sat

Left
DRIVEN GROUSE
Watercolour

Right
DRIVEN GROUSE SKETCH
Pencil

shivering for over four hours and saw nothing. I could hear them, that extraordinary climactic call, but not a glimpse of the bird. The next morning was a different matter however.

It is always magical to watch the first glimmerings of light start a new day, and from the secrecy of my hide I watched as the shapes of trees distinguished themselves from the darkness, when with a great flapping of wings, a huge cock capercaillie flew down from the trees and commenced his display. And what a display. Head thrown back, body quivering as he made that extraordinary noise, and every now and again his huge wings thumping the still air, he would perform great 'flutter jumps'. He was a dominant male and looked very proud of his harem. One would have thought that as an alpha male he would have been a pristine example of his kind, but it was obvious from the missing patches of feathers around his head and neck, and the scratches around his eyes that he had earned his position the hard way! It was quite a challenge to try and sketch him in the cramped semi-dark hide. I made him look a little smarter in any pieces I did of him afterwards! I have been fortunate to see some of the great wildlife sights this world has to offer, from great bustards in Spain to the wild game of Botswana, but that half-lit display ranks with the most thrilling! What a privilege. For those few hours I was transported back to an altogether wilder age.

~Black Grouse~

I'm showing off now. Not only do I have red grouse by my house, I have black game too. Every morning in the spring I stand at the window with a cup of tea and my binoculars and count how many cocks are on the lek. If it is a still morning then as I let the dogs out of the kennel I can hear the bubbling, hissing calls of black grouse displaying. I have on a few occasions had black game displaying and feeding less than twenty feet from my studio!

It's always a pleasure taking people out to watch the lek, one of our most spectacular wildlife sights. It is wonderful to watch the posturing, the staccato dashes back and forth and the fluttering leaps into the air as the cocks try to attract the favours of the hens. What strikes a lot of people seeing blackcocks for the first time is quite how blue the colouring is on the cocks when the light hits them right. The combination of the blue, the large red wattle, the handsome black lyre-shaped tail and the snowy under tail makes him a favorite subject for many artists. The other surprise for watchers unfamiliar with these birds is their activity in trees, but they spend quite a lot of time off the ground. However they aren't the most agile of birds, and there is a deal of overbalancing and wing waving as they feed in the birches and rowans. Another thing about blackcock that surprises people is that apart from when they're moulting, they lek throughout the year. Not maybe as dramatically as in the spring, but as I write this it's nearly November and there were five cocks lekking behind the cottage this morning.

I have done many studies of blackcocks and as with the red grouse, I enjoy showing the less well shown part of their life as well as the famous and beautiful display. One morning despite having other work I needed to be getting on with, I had to take the time to sketch a blackcock feeding on buttercup heads out of my bathroom window!

With a little care and thought we might manage to preserve these magical birds, so their spectacular courtship dance and mysterious calls can still thrill the watcher in the wild and lonely dawn.

FOOTNOTE *In the time I have been compiling these thoughts about grouse my old Labrador bitch has taken ill, and I had to have her put down. I can't imagine how many grouse she's retrieved to me in her career. I buried her under the heather within view of the house. As I laid her in the ground the only sound other than the wind coming over the moor was 'Go back, go back, go back, go back- back- back- back- back- back- back- back- back...' She couldn't have had a better salute.*

Clockwise from right
HISSING & FLUTTER JUMP
Watercolour
BLACKCOCKS IN TREES
Watercolour
BLACK GROUSE IN TREES
Pencil

Left
COCK CAPERCAILLIE DISPLAY

Below
BLACKCOCKS LEKKING IN FROST
Watercolour

Right and below
SKETCH BOOK PAGES
Watercolour

Above
BLACKCOCK IN FROST STUDY
Watercolour

Clockwise from top left
GROUSE IN HEATHER

GROUSE CREEPING
THROUGH HEATHER

DRIVEN GROUSE STUDY
Watercolour

Right
DISPLAYING GROUSE STUDY
Watercolour

Below
COCK GROUSE ON WALL
Watercolour

Left
IN THE PINK
Oil on canvas

Derek Robertson

MOORLAND CAN SEEM bleak, uninspiring and forbidding, but it has a beauty and a fascination all of its own: in dramatic mountain panoramas and in the microcosm of habitats that make up the miniature landscapes at your feet. But their fascination goes further, for every landscape tells a story.

No other bird is so identified with the Scottish moors as the red grouse and the British race was considered, until 1952, to be an entirely separate species from the willow grouse, whose range stretches across the higher latitudes in a broad swathe that encircles the arctic regions across the globe. Now designated as a subspecies of the willow grouse, it retains the label *'scoticus'*, which still indicates the special relationship that the grouse has with heather moorland and, by association, with the physical and cultural landscape of Scotland.

That association has a straightforward cause: red grouse eat heather, almost exclusively, throughout the year. They depend so completely on heather as a food source that they are almost never seen away from this habitat unless driven to lower ground by extreme weather and heavy falls of snow. The heather moor itself is divided up into territories by the male grouse from autumn onwards and is defended by him, and later with the help of his mate, against neighbouring birds, until the chicks hatch in the spring. The breeding density varies depending on the quantity and quality of heather available and if a male bird cannot defend a territory he is excluded into marginal habitat. These birds do not survive the winter.

When you are walking through the moors, you will cross from one territory to the next flushing up individuals or pairs of birds that own that territory. They call and scold at one another from the tops of rocks and scurry about in heated, scrabbling fights over the boundaries of their petty kingdoms, then preen and strut among the heather. The Scottish Highlanders recognised the combative and territorial pretensions of these birds and naturally assumed that their calls were something akin to the Gaelic slogans that would be cried by clansmen in battle. They believe that the Grouse shout, *'Cò, cò, cò, cò, mo chlaidheamh, mo chlaidheamh, mo chlaidheamh'*, which translates as 'Who, who, who, who (is there), (fetch) my sword, my sword'.

The heather moors that cover large areas of the

Highlands are not a natural habitat. On areas of blanket bog and the high hillsides, tracts of heather moorland would have survived from the end of the last ice age, but much of the open ground we see today was covered by forest. This was cleared by man. In the Highlands, this was for timber, and to clear ground for grazing, and even to clear out packs of wolves and bands of thieves. This went further with the successive development of sheep farming and deer shooting as a source of income on estates, which

eat the next year. In well managed areas, this results in a mosaic of habitats of different heights and a patchwork of patterns stretching over the hills where you can see areas of black ground that have just been burnt next to green patches of new growth and areas of brown heather of different heights from previous seasons. Walking through a grouse moor, one often crosses a patch of burned heather where your boots stir up puffs of ash and crunch through the charred stalks of heather which scratch your ankles and

Right
MUIRBURN
STUDIES I & II
Watercolour

Opposite
GROUSE PORTRAIT
Gouache on paper

led to increased grazing and the suppression of natural regeneration where any new saplings were simply grazed out. The result is a habitat where the 'climax' vegetation is heather: a woody plant that forms a forest up to eighteen inches high, and is interspersed with grasses and low herbage. As man removed the forests, the grouse increased their range. Many estates, particularly those that managed their land for deer, began to manage their ground for grouse too.

Heather is often managed by successive burning, where patches of ground are burned one year to encourage new, fresh growth and plenty of heather shoots for the grouse to

scribble charcoal lines across the bottoms of your trousers. Often the ground is littered with the cocoons of moths, sometimes hundreds at a time, scattered like oversized ant-eggs among the black sticks. You may cross an area like this in the following summer when the heather shoots have grown through and the lush growth has attracted not only grouse but numerous insects and consequently the small birds that feed on them. These areas are particularly rich in wildlife and the low vegetation makes it easier to see things like moths, lizards and snakes, but it is good too for some ground nesting birds that like open spaces such as lapwing, oystercatcher and sometimes even gulls.

However the old, deep vegetation is very important too, because it provides cover for the grouse and other species of birds, both as shelter in the winter and for nesting.

A consequence of this management is that all tree saplings are eliminated. There is no regeneration of forest and this land use has contributed significantly to the open landscape and extensive moorland habitats, with their associated wildlife, that we think of as typical of the Scottish Highlands today. In a sense, much of the wildlife that we find interesting in Scotland, the particular range of moorland flora and fauna, is maintained by the management of ground for a combination of grouse, red deer and sheep. It is not surprising then that grouse have also had a cultural impact in the Scottish Highlands where they have generated a significant level of income and employment. The Scottish estates boast a range of buldings from castles and palaces to shooting lodges and primitive bothies that have been built to accommodate landowners, shooting guests and keepers. Grouse butts are ranged across the hillsides and road links and even railway lines have been developed to service some of these estates. The driven grouse drive and the first brace sent south to

London are now considered traditional manifestations of Scottish culture.

The effects of sporting patronage are not always benign, and the consequence of maintaining so much grouse moor has been a loss of native forests and natural diversity. The control of predators to generate high numbers of grouse has depleted bird of prey populations and this issue continues to generate controversy today. Although the development of grouse moors came late in the history of Highland land use, it is often widely perceived to be part of a system of clearance and patronage that exploited and removed the native population and devastated their native, Gaelic culture. In reality, change of land use to grouse moor had little large-scale effect, especially in comparison to sheep, deer, famine and other economic factors, but as late as 1916, G. S. Bruce wrote in the *Highland News* about the Duke of Sutherland's efforts to evict an eighty-three year-old man from his holding at Cnocan to make way for grouse moor. Although instances like this rarely occurred over the development of grouse moor, they followed a pattern of evictions that cut deep into the Highland psyche. However, by the time the grouse moors were established, most of the people had been evicted already to make way for sheep or deer.

The grouse moors and the heather-covered hills are the legacy of this protracted history, and they are spectacular to visit. They have the immense, solitary feel of wild places, which some of them certainly are, and the landscape they occupy is inhabited by a fascinating range of plants and wild creatures: wild flowers, dragonflies, butterflies, birds, lizards, ferns and grasses. At the height of summer, the moor is threaded with a myriad of wild flowers and, as the season begins to tip into late summer, the heather begins to bloom. First the bell heather in brooding purple patches, and then the ling blossoms across the hillside, suffusing the entire panorama with a radiant blush of pink that seems to glow with a light of its own: so bright and intense that you imagine that you can hear it buzzing with colour – and then you realise that you really are hearing something: the buzz of millions of insects drawn by the abundance of nectar swelling in each of the tiny flower heads. Hoverflies and bumble bees crawl and dodder over the petals and honey bees range across the hillsides, often many miles from the hives that have been brought up from the lowlands especially to exploit this natural bonanza.

Among all of this, the grouse strut around, both the adult birds and the fully grown chicks. They nibble at the heather, eating the shoots and flowers; sometimes snapping at the passing insects, or pecking at the ripening blaeberries. The territories have broken down, and family parties join up into loose flocks, but they still give the impression that they are tending the hillsides, carefully gardening and picking at the fruits of summer, or standing dumpy and immobile, sun-struck, looking like votive pots, their necks pointing up at the sun; left as half-remembered offerings by a Neolithic cult, relict guardians of the heather moors.

At this time of year too, you might see birds dust-bathing. They prefer to find patches of dry, sun-parched, sandy soil which they can flap amongst and stir up into their feathers. They fluff out like turkey-cocks to sift the sand through every quill and scour over their skin. Often they stop, half way through, eyes shut in rapture and wings fanned out, absorbing the hot summer sunshine. It often seems to be a social occasion, with several birds bathing together. Always one appears to be hanging back, perched high up and looking about warily: presumably on sentry duty. Birds on the edge of the patch of sand peck around and pick up pieces of grit and pebble to aid digestion. The sentry is a good idea. Lots of creatures, not just people, think that grouse make a

tasty meal. If they are amongst good cover and think they haven't been seen, the grouse will flatten out and try to hide from view of a bird of prey. If the predator gets too close, they may panic and once one or two grouse flush, the whole flock goes up in a blurring throng, weaving and whirring off as fast as possible. They can fly quickly, and if they are in a flock, they can often avoid most birds of prey if they see them first. Their real danger is when they are preoccupied, when dust-bathing for example, and are ambushed by an eagle appearing suddenly over a rise, or are stooped on at spectacularly high speed by a peregrine.

The croak and clatter of the grouse often continues through the night, particularly during the short summer nights and when the moon is full. After dark, you may hear them calling; defending territories and squabbling over their boundaries, or the whinny of wings and cackle of alarm when they are disturbed by deer or foxes. On a bright night, when your eyes have become accustomed to the gloom, a walk through the wild moors can be an exhilarating experience and gives you an altogether more primeval encounter with a wild landscape. A fall of snow can give you a similar impression when the landscape seems to return to a pristine state. The horizons are narrowed down and all traces of human activity seem to disappear. You begin to get some impression of just how difficult this environment can be to survive in – the grouse, of course, have no choice. In really bad weather they try to sit out the storms, huddled together and burrowed down into the snow. They search over the windswept ridges to find exposed heather shoots and kick up the snow to feed on the vegetation beneath. It is in these conditions that they can be seen on lower ground, one of the few occasions when they might be forced off their natural habitat. When snow lies deep in drifts, they may actually migrate uphill, into the domain of ptarmigan and mountain hares, onto the few places where fierce winds have swept the vegetation clear of snow.

To some people, grouse are a challenge in themselves, a quarry to pursue, to study, observe, to paint, or a resource to manage. To others they are an excuse to experience the high moors. They are certainly an intrinsic part of the Highland landscape, part of the essence of these high places that inspire and restore the human spirit.

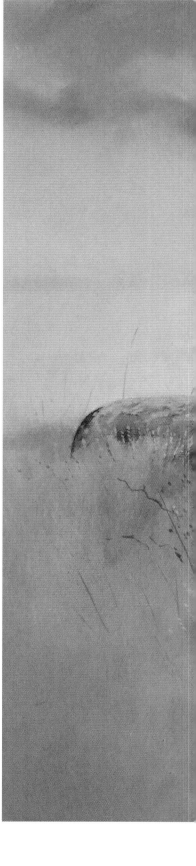

Left
EVENING LIGHT
Gouache on linen

Right
AMONG THE BUZZING BELLS
Gouache on paper

Right
PUNK GROUSE
Gouache on linen

Opposite
SETTING THE HEATHER ALIGHT
Oil on canvas

Above
MIDNIGHT ON THE HILLS
Watercolour

Right
GROUSE BY MOONLIGHT
Gouache on paper

Above
THERE MAY BE SNOW
Watercolour

Left
THE HIGH GROUND
Oil on canvas

Right
SNOWBOUND
Watercolour monochrome

THE ARTISTS

Keith Sykes

Keith was born in Morecambe, Lancashire in 1957 and continues to live there with his family.

At an early age his father introduced him to various aspects of shooting. Wildfowling, rough shooting, clay pigeon and rifle shooting in his early teens formed the foundation of his love of the sport. From ancestral links back to professional punt gunners on the Essex coast, the family tradition and love of the sport has now been passed to the next generation and inherited by Keith's two sons, Jack and Tom.

Whilst at school in his early teens Keith began to paint and draw wildfowl. This was particularly influenced and inspired by the work of Sir Peter Scott.

On leaving full time education Keith embarked on a career in civil engineering, eventually making a transition to detailed design in both civil engineering and building construction. Many of his early years were spent producing fine detailed architectural work on a drawing board but, with the introduction of CAD, drawing board skills became a thing of the past. Keith's latter years in the construction industry were focused on the project management of building and engineering schemes for the NHS.

Combining his drawing board experience with a passion for shooting and gun dogs he now concentrates on producing finely detailed animal portraits. Specialising in sporting dogs but portraying all breeds as well as horses and wildlife, he works exclusively in black and white on scraperboard.

Keen for an active involvement in conservation, he has served on the Executive Committee of the Morecambe Bay Wildfowlers' Association since the 1970s and has been the Secretary of the Wyre-Lune Sanctuary Committee since 1991.

As with many artists, photography has formed an integral part of capturing reference material, Keith is never without a camera on shoot days and his photographs often appear in the sporting press. His artwork is often featured too and in 2004 he was commissioned to produce the cover of the Christmas Edition of The Field magazine.

www.kjsykes.com

Simon Gudgeon *ARBS SWLA*

Scratch the surface of any wildlife artist and you soon realise that they all share a passion and almost schoolboy-like enthusiasm for what they do. It comes from deep within and most have had it since their earliest days – you could almost say from the cradle.

So it is with Simon Gudgeon – this country's leading contemporary wildlife sculptor. His earliest days were spent on the family farm in Yorkshire learning the essential arts of observation, evaluation, interpretation – how animals and birds behave with each other and

in the presence of man. Learning to understand the importance of balance in nature and man's impact – good and bad. So it is in his blood, and since those early years his interest and zeal has increased, been refined and honed and with it his artistic talents.

Simon Gudgeon's signature style is instantly recognisable – a smooth, minimalised form expressing in simple lines both movement and emotion. A moment captured. He is particularly admired for his sculpture of birds in flight and the ingenious engineering of bases which seem to launch the bird into air rather than anchor it to the ground.

His latest work strongly favours an even more pared down approach to wildlife sculpture with inspiration springing from the smallest of details – the curve of a beak, the angle of the neck – and then moulded into a form which suggests rather than dictates a particular bird or mammal.

His greatest inspiration will always spring from observing in the wild. Simon believes that before you can sculpt a creature, you have to understand it and where it comes from. Relating creatures to their natural habitat and how they live within it are one of his passions.

www.simongudgeon.com
sg@simongudgeon.com

Ben Hoskyns

Born in 1963, Ben spent most of his childhood in East Anglia where he now lives with his wife and two sons.

He adored painting as a young child but his art master at school offered him little encouragement and he gave up before 'O' Levels although he continued to 'scribble' from time to time – his subjects invariably being birds.

After several years in insurance, getting nowhere in particular, Ben decided that he had to move on. Stubbornly ignoring any well-intended suggestions that he should, perhaps, get some training first, he started to paint for a living in 1988. He had been fascinated by wildlife from early childhood and never seriously considered painting anything else once he turned professional.

Concentrating generally on British wildlife and on game birds in particular, Ben finds no shortage of inspiration whether at home in Suffolk, knee-deep in snipe bogs in Devon or dodging midges on grouse moors in Northumberland. His landscapes are, quite simply, about the feeling of 'being there' and his studies capture the very essence of the subject.

Ben wrote and illustrated Holland & Holland's The Nature of Game (Quiller Press 1994) and has illustrated several other books, numerous magazine articles and his paintings have been used as Christmas cards by both The Game Conservancy Trust and The Countryside Alliance. He produced the jacket paintings for two of The Game Conservancy Trust's Annual Reviews and for the front cover of the 2005 Scottish Game Fair programme and was commissioned to paint the 2006 Wildlife Habitat Trust UK Habitat Conservation Stamp.

www.benhoskyns.com

Terence Lambert

Born in 1951. Terence lived in the Surrey countryside where his countryman father lit the flame of a burning passion for the natural world, and encouraged his precocious drawing talent.

His first book Lambert's Birds of Garden and Woodland (Collins 1976) was published in eight languages, and established his career. He has contributed to over forty books and part works since then and many more limited edition prints. His commissions and international exhibitions have taken him all over the world. In 1999 the Welsh Arts Council supported a major retrospective. One hundred and sixty works were exhibited, showing in venues through out the principality.

He moved to Mid Wales with his young family in 1976 where he still lives today, gaining an endless supply of inspiration from the diversity of the Welsh landscape. Although a very disciplined artist his love for his one acre garden, and fly fishing, will frequently lure him from the studio.

Rodger McPhail

Rodger McPhail was born in Lancashire in 1953. He studied graphic design at Liverpool School of Art. While still at college, he was introduced to Aylmer Tryon, and so began a long association with The Tryon Gallery in London.

Over the years, Rodger has contributed to many mixed exhibitions at the gallery and has had twelve one-man shows.

One of the great perks of Rodger's work is that it has taken him all over the world, and enabled him to enjoy some of the finest shooting and fishing available.

As well as sporting and wildlife painting, Rodger also does cartoons, caricatures, portraits and stage sets.

He has illustrated over twenty books, including two of his own, Open Season and Fishing Season (Swan Hill Press).

Rodger McPhail lives in the Lune Valley, Lancashire with his wife Cecilia, and his sons, Gavin and Alastair.

Jonathan Sainsbury

Jonathan was born in Stratford upon Avon in 1951 and grew up in rural Warwickshire. He was fascinated by nature from the start. He went to art college at Leamington Spa and the Byam Shaw School and worked in the scenery painting department of the Royal Shakespeare Theatre, before graduating from Leeds College of Art. He has painted full-time ever since.

He has exhibited several times at 'Birds in Art' at the Leigh Yawkey Woodson Art Museum, Wisconsin. The gallery bought his picture The Game Larder for its permanent collection and toured his works round the United States and Europe. He won the Maude Gemmell Hutchison prize at the Scottish Royal Academy. He was a prize winner in the BASC painting competition. He was in the Sunday Times/Singer & Friedlander watercolour exhibition. His work is on loan to the Society of Wildlife Artists in Nature, Gloucester.

For many years he has sold through the major sporting and wildlife galleries, has exhibited at the Society of Wildlife Artists and contributed to numerous events supporting The Game Conservancy Trust.

Email: info@jonathansainsbury.com
www.jonathansainsbury.com

Owen Williams

Owen Williams spent his childhood years growing up on a hill farm in West Wales where he enjoyed long summer hours stalking the overgrown banks of his local stream fishing for wild brown trout, and in the winter months shooting snipe, duck and pigeon on his home ground.

It was during these early years that he first started drawing the wildlife that he found so fascinating. He speaks with passion about a particular evening flighting teal with a homemade decoy and how on his return home he set about depicting the moment in a drawing, the result was his first sporting picture.

On leaving school Owen moved to London to follow a career in advertising working for a major publishing company and although away from the countryside, his fishing and shooting, he continued to work at his artistic skills.

In 1985 he decided to return to Cardiganshire with his wife Sally and young family to become a full time artist. Many of his early paintings sold into the US through the London Gallery of H C Dickins, and in more recent years he has become established as one of the country's leading sporting artists. Working exclusively in watercolour his paintings contain a strong element of landscape and weather, which help to convey a real feeling of time and place.

In 2003 Owen Williams was commissioned by the Royal Household to paint a picture as a twenty-first birthday present for HRH Prince William which now hangs in Clarence House. Over the years his work has been included in many major collections of sporting and wildlife art in the country. His pictures have been published in many wildlife books and the sporting press, and he is a member of the design panel of the Welsh Books Council. In 2001 he was commissioned by BASC to design their Wildlife Habitat Trust stamp.

www.owenwilliams.org.uk
wildscapes_2000@yahoo.co.uk

Ashley Boon

Ashley Boon was born in London in 1959, but grew up in rural Northamptonshire. He trained at Banbury School of Art and gained a BA (Hons) in Illustration at Bristol. He now lives in Cumbria with his wife and daughter.

Like many wildlife artists it was his love of natural history which came first, and his early paintings were mostly of birds and animals. He sold his first painting at the age of fourteen.

As a young man he rode to hounds with the Grafton Hunt, and when he was able he pursued his interest in falconry. As an art student he shared his Bristol bedsit with a goshawk. He is too busy these days to devote the time required to hawking, but he is a keen shot, stalker and fly fisherman. These interests are naturally reflected in his work and he was pleased to be described once as an artist who 'practises what he paints'.

As well as enjoying painting our native wildlife, he has more recently been drawn to Africa, where a boyhood fascination has become a passion. He now leads annual bird watching safaris to the Okavango Delta area in Botswana.

His work has been used as Christmas cards for the BASC and also the Game Conservancy Trust with whom he is a regular exhibitor at the CLA Game Fair. He has illustrated several books and part works including The Pigeon Shooter by John Batley (Swan Hill), Private Thoughts from a Small Shoot by Lawrence Catlow (Merlin Unwin Books) and Muntjac, Managing an Alien Species by Charles Smith-Jones (Coch-y-Bonddu Books).

www.ashleyboon.co.uk
ashley.boon@btopenworld.com

Derek Robertson

Derek Robertson works from his studio in Aberdeen and, since graduating from Duncan of Jordanstone Art College in Dundee some fifteen years ago, has established a name as one of the country's foremost wildlife and landscape artists. He exhibits work in galleries around the world including regular selection in the Woodson Art Museum 'Birds in Art' international show in the USA. His paintings are held in private collections in more than 40 countries as well as in numerous public collections including those of several British universities, museums and the collections of HRH the Duke of Edinburgh and The Scotland Office in London. Derek is a professional member of the Society of Scottish Artists.

He is regularly featured in press, and on radio and television. His first book, Highland Sketchbook *was nominated for the McVities Prize. He has written and presented a number of TV programmes including a four-part series,* Drawn From Wild Places *which was nominated for a Scottish Bafta and an award at the Cannes Film Festival. His latest book, entitled* A Studio Under The Sky *has received critical acclaim from around the world. He illustrated the bestselling books* Song of the Rolling Earth *and* Nature's Child *written by Sir John Lister-Kaye. Derek regularly gives talks and demonstrations about his work, the landscape, and the wildlife that he portrays. These include prestigious presentations such as the Armistead Lecture and programmes for cruise lines.*

As well as having a fascination for wildlife as an artist, Derek contributes to scientific research work as an enthusiastic amateur naturalist, researcher and bird-bander. He has developed a number of research and survey techniques that have been adopted by professional organizations. He has had his researches published in numerous scientific journals, been author and editor in many publications and serves as a volunteer on several research and trust committees.

Email: derekart@btinternet.com
Website: www.derekrobertson.com